SPEAK
PEACE
IN A
WORLD OF
CONFLICT

SPEAK
PEACE
IN A
WORLD OF
CONFLICT

What **You** Say Next
Will Change **Your** World

by Marshall B. Rosenberg, Ph.D.

PuddleDancer
PRESS

P.O. Box 231129, Encinitas, CA 92023-1129
email@PuddleDancer.com • www.PuddleDancer.com

For additional information:
Center for Nonviolent Communication, 2428 Foothill Blvd., Suite E, La Crescenta, CA 91214
Tel: 818-957-9393 • Fax: 818-957-1424 • E-mail: cnvc@CNVC.org • Website: www.CNVC.org

PuddleDancer Press, Permissions Dept.
P.O. Box 231129, Encinitas, CA 92023-1129
Fax: 1-858-759-6967, email@PuddleDancer.com

Author: Marshall B. Rosenberg, Ph.D.

Manuscript Development: Graham Van Dixhorn,
Write to Your Market, Inc., www.WriteToYourMarket.com

Editor: Dan Shenk, CopyProof, ShenkCopyProof@aol.com

Index: Phyllis Linn, Indexpress

Cover and interior design: Lightbourne, Inc.,
www.lightbourne.com

Cover photograph: www.gettyimages.com

Manufactured in the United States of America

10 9 8 7 6 5 4 3 2 1

Library of Congress Cataloging-in-Publication Data

Rosenberg, Marshall B.
    Speak peace : what you say next will change your world / by Marshall B.
Rosenberg.—1st ed.
        p. cm.
    Includes bibliographical references and index.
    ISBN-13: 978-1-892005-17-5 (pbk. : alk. paper)
    1. Interpersonal communication. 2. Interpersonal relations. I. Title.
BF637.C45R648 2005
303.6'9—dc22
                                         2005017819

Praise for *Speak Peace in a World of Conflict*

"*Speak Peace* is a book that comes at an appropriate time when anger and violence dominate human attitudes. Marshall Rosenberg gives us the means to create peace through our speech and communication. A brilliant book."

— ARUN GANDHI, president, M.K. Gandhi
Institute for Nonviolence, USA

"*Speak Peace* sums up decades of healing and peacework. It would be hard to list all the kinds of people who can benefit from reading this book, because it's really any and all of us."

— DR. MICHAEL NAGLER, author, *America Without Violence* and
Is There No Other Way: The Search for a Nonviolent Future

"*Speak Peace* is set apart from the fine body of literature on the subject of nonviolence by its fundamental intimacy with the complexities of human nature. Rosenberg brings us globally critical evidence that how and what we speak reflects who we are and embodies what we will become."

— DR. BARBARA E. FIELDS, executive director,
The Association for Global New Thought

"Many books on communication are strong on theory but impractical on application. Marshall Rosenberg's instant classic is the stand out exception. It is clear and compelling in its logic and flat-out inspiring in its inviting exposition of usable techniques and strategies. If enough people read this book, the world will transform."

— HUGH PRATHER, author, *The Little Book of
Letting Go, Shining Through*, and *Morning Notes*

"*Speak Peace in a World of Conflict* offers a gift of spirit, theory and nonviolent communication experience from which every seeker of peace within and without can learn. It complements John Burton's *Deviance, Terrorism and War* as a guide to mutual need-fulfilling processes of problem-solving to realize nonviolent conditions of global life."

— GLENN D. PAIGE, author, *Nonkilling Global Political Science*;
founder, Center for Global Nonviolence

"*Speak Peace* demonstrates how we can make our deepest yearnings for a harmonious world come true. Through stories and exercises, this book shows us simple yet subtle practices for creating peace—internally, externally, and institutionally. If you want to do your bit to create a happier world, get fluent in this process!"

— DIANA LION, associate director and prison
program director, Buddhist Peace Fellowship

CONTENTS

ACKNOWLEDGMENTS

WHEN I STARTED OUT MORE THAN 30 YEARS AGO, I HAD TO look hard to find people with the ability to imagine the way the world could be—and the energy and skills to create the social change needed. Nowadays it's easier. I feel encouraged to see Nonviolent Communication spreading as a grassroots movement by people getting trained in NVC, then connecting with people in other countries and training them to train others. These people are what give me hope, and they're not hard to find in any country.

I see a different world than most people do on television. I work in many of these same places that are in the news, such as Sierra Leone, Sri Lanka, Burundi, Bosnia and Serbia, Colombia, and the Middle East as well. I've worked in both Rwanda and Nigeria with people who have had everybody in their family killed, so I know what can happen in this world.

But all over the world I work with people who tell me it doesn't have to be that way. I work with people who have a different world view, a different consciousness, and these people are spreading their consciousness very rapidly. Their courage, their vision, and their ability to keep their energy up-under even the most difficult circumstances-inspire me beyond words.

I'm grateful that I was able to study and work with Professor Carl Rogers at a time when he was researching the components of helping relationships. The results of this research played a key role in the evolution of the process of communication that I describe in this book.

I would like to express gratitude to my friend Annie Muller. Her encouragement to be clearer about the spiritual foundations

1

of my work has strengthened that work and enriched my life.

I will be forever grateful that Professor Michael Hakeem helped me see the scientific limitations and the social and political dangers of a pathology-based understanding of human beings. Seeing the limitations of this model stimulated me to search for a model of psychology based on a growing clarity about how we human beings are meant to live.

I am especially grateful for those whom I call NVC breeders, people who have committed their lives to spreading the consciousness of NVC. The following is a brief list of people to whom I feel grateful for their instrumental role in spreading NVC during the early days in different areas throughout the world.

NAFEZ ASSAILY *in Palestine*

ANNE BOURRIT *in Switzerland*

BOB CONDE *in Sierra Leone*

VILMA COSTETTI *in Italy*

DUNIA HATEGEKIMANA *in Burundi*

RITA HERZOG *in USA*

NADA IGNJATOVIC-SAVIC *in Yugoslavia*

SAMIE IHEJIRKA *in Nigeria*

BARBARA KUNZ *in Switzerland*

JEAN-FRANCOIS LECOQ *in Belgium*

LUCY LEU *in USA*

PASCALE MOLO *in France*

THEODORE MUKUDONGA *in Rwanda*

SISTER CARMEL NELAND *in Ireland*

CHRIS RAJENDRAM *in Sri Lanka*

JORGE RUBIO *in Colombia*

TOWE WIDSTRAND *in Sweden*

And there are so many, many others, more than I can list here. It is a source of great joy to me to see how these individuals, along with thousands of others, are contributing to peace in their communities, in their local regions, in their countries, and now throughout the world.

— MARSHALL B. ROSENBERG, PH.D.

FOREWORD

DOROTHY J. MAVER, PH.D.

SOUND IS A POWERFUL CREATIVE AGENT. OUR SPEECH REFLECTS our thoughts and perceptions, defining the world in which we live.

It is through our speech that we are known, for it tells a story of our thought life and essential self. How we speak can open or close doors, heal or hurt, create joy or suffering, and ultimately determines our own degree of happiness.

When I first heard Marshall Rosenberg speak peace, I knew I had been introduced to a man with a vision and the courage to act on that vision. As he shared his humorous and profound perspective and real-life stories about how lives were changed because everyone's needs were met, he affirmed what I already knew in my heart. It *is* possible to live in right relationship with one another and all life.

In this time of pain and suffering in our world, Marshall gives us a key. This key unlocks the gift of understanding as to how our use of speech impacts and influences our lives and the lives of others. He offers concrete examples, a depth of knowledge, and a plethora of tools to bring harmony through conflict in any situation where there is willingness to participate.

Evaluating a Nonviolent Communication Workshop for political activists, a participant shared the relief and hope experienced as anger shifted and resolved. In the past, her angry way of communicating had kept her from being an effective political activist and change agent.

As we learn to speak peace in a world of conflict, we transform the world we live in, becoming a cause and not simply an effect. Our speech helps create a world that works for everyone, a world in which we understand and live the concept of Nonviolent Communication. Living intentionally in this way our motivations are transformed, and we come to know what Marshall means when he says, "… actions are taken for the sole purpose of willingly contributing to the well-being of others and ourselves."

Speak Peace is so much more than a self-help book. You will come away from this book knowing how to participate effectively in personal, social, political, and global change. This book is excellent and so needed at this juncture in our evolution. Peace begins with each one of us. Thank you, Marshall Rosenberg for a significant contribution to building a Culture of Peace.

— DOROTHY J. MAVER, PH.D.
is Executive Director of The Peace Alliance and
The Peace Alliance Foundation, educating for
a Culture of Peace and advocating for a US
Department of Peace. www.ThePeaceAlliance.org

FOREWORD

DAVID HART,

Washington, DC, July 2005

A S I SIT DOWN TO WRITE THIS FOREWORD ABOUT THE importance of Nonviolent Communication, the world is still reeling from the bombings on the London subway on July 7, 2005. We awoke to learn that "it" had happened again. We saw the sights and heard the sounds of violence and felt a deep personal connection to those who were suffering and whose loved ones are suffering still.

Somehow, across the miles that separate us from the site of the bombings, we grasped the pain that violence brings. Once again we saw the reality that bombs destroy fragile human forms and rip apart lives of valuable human beings. Though distance could provide a cushion to the shock, instead, in Washington, DC, and throughout the United States and the world, we sensed the crushing power of fear.

As I celebrate the tools of Nonviolent Communication presented in the work you hold in your hands, I wonder what it will take to truly "speak peace in a world of conflict." The violence that shocked us on July 7, 2005, is all too common, too familiar, too much a part of our lives. Sometimes we recognize our connection to those who are affected by this pandemic of violence. Mostly, we seem to go numb—unable to either feel the pain of violence or the beauty of our shared humanity.

The day before the London bombings, lives were ripped apart in Baghdad and Fallujah. We participated in this violence, but we failed to mourn those victims or to ask when it will end. We only tend to notice if those whose lives are snuffed out prematurely are seen to be "like us." If they wear the right uniform or look "like us," we recognize our common experience and see them as fully human. If not, we may fail to grasp the value of their lives.

In this important book, Dr. Rosenberg reminds us that, "we've been living under this destructive mythology for a long time, and it comes complete with a language that dehumanizes people and turns them into objects." Moreover, he offers us a suggested path out of this darkness. He reminds us that what you say and do matters. Our actions and our failure to act in the face of growing violence shapes the world and determines our future.

In my position with the Association for Conflict Resolution, I have the great pleasure of working with skilled professionals who strive every day to help people resolve conflicts in a manner that is creative, constructive, and does not resort to violence. As practitioners in the expanding and vital field of Conflict Resolution, our members recognize conflict as a natural and healthy part of life. We would never seek to eliminate conflict, because we believe that conflict can help us grow as individuals and as societies. Instead, we seek a more effective response to conflict. Dr. Rosenberg offers us a creative approach to communication in a world awash in violence.

I celebrate the pragmatic visionaries who seek a better world and work every day to bring that world into being. Through our collaboration, we may just find a path that brings us from the darkness of violence to the light of peace. Dr. Rosenberg has added his thoughtful voice to an important conversation. His approach is insightful, provocative, and is sure to spark discussion. While his presentation doesn't exactly match my approach, that is not the point. He would not want simple agreement. He wants to engage us in a vital dialogue that allows us to look within and ask ourselves what role we can play in making the world a better place.

Nonviolent Communication is part of the solution to the problems we face today. As I brace myself to enter the subway here in Washington, DC, I am strengthened by the work of Dr. Rosenberg and those like him all around the world who are not willing to accept the status quo of violent responses to conflict.

Read this book, take its message to heart, and let it be a step in a life-long journey of self-discovery and peacemaking. Together, bit by bit, word by word, day by day, we can truly "Speak Peace in a World of Conflict" and by so doing we can build a brighter future.

— DAVID A. HART
*is Chief Executive Officer of the Association
for Conflict Resolution (ACR)*

(*Title for identification purposes only, not endorsed by ACR*)

INTRODUCTION

*"We need a more peaceful world,
growing out of more peaceful families and
neighborhoods and communities. To secure and
cultivate such peace, we must love others, even
our enemies as well as our friends."*

—HOWARD W. HUNTER

I AM GRATEFUL FOR THE OPPORTUNITY TO SHARE WITH YOU the purpose and principles of Nonviolent Communication (NVC) and give you examples of how it's being used by people throughout the world on a number of different levels. I'll show you how it's being used within ourselves, as well as how it's used to create quality connections with others at home, at work, and in efforts toward social change.

Speaking peace is communicating without violence, the practical outcome of applying the principles of Nonviolent Communication. It is a giving and a receiving of messages that center on two very important questions: *What's alive in us?* and *What can we do to make life more wonderful?*

Speaking peace is a way of connecting with others that allows our natural compassion to flourish. Around the world—from troubled families to dysfunctional bureaucracies

9

to war-ravaged countries—I've found no more effective means of getting to a peaceful resolution of conflict. In fact, speaking peace using Nonviolent Communication offers the promise of reducing or even eliminating conflict in the first place.

Bringing about peaceful change begins with working on our own mindsets.

For most of us the process of bringing about peaceful change begins with working on our own mindsets, on the way we view ourselves and others, on the way we get our needs met. This basic work is in many ways the most challenging aspect of speaking peace because it requires great honesty and openness, developing a certain literacy of expression, and overcoming deeply ingrained learning that emphasizes judgment, fear, obligation, duty, punishment and reward, and shame. It may not be easy, but the results are worth the effort.

Part I of this book focuses on the mechanics of the process of NVC by posing two basic questions, the answers to which not only form an excellent overview of NVC but will also give you a sense of the differences between NVC and your current understanding of how to resolve differences. Applying NVC to your life, to your relationships, and to your broader efforts toward peaceful resolution of conflict will almost certainly involve some fairly significant changes in how you view the world and operate within it.

Everything we do is in service of our needs.

For example, one basic concept in NVC—that everything we do is in service of our needs—has no corollary in mainstream thinking. When this one concept is applied to our view of others, we'll see that we have no real enemies, that what others do to us is the best possible thing they know to do to get their needs met.

We can help them see more effective, less damaging ways to do it, but we don't blame them, shame them, or hate them for not being what we want them to be. Far from leaving us powerless or requiring us to overpower others to get our needs met, speaking peace with NVC employs a tactic we call "power with."

Part II of this book discusses changes that take place in ourselves, in our view of others, and in how we view the world when our motivation is to enrich life.

Part III supports your attempts at speaking peace by providing more advanced feedback on applying NVC to social change. I encourage you to team up with others who have similar values, to talk about how to do that, and to share thoughts on how to get your needs met when dealing with people who are less than receptive to your efforts.

In addition to what might be called "political" change, we'll also look at applying NVC to other areas of society, such as business or school settings. It's no coincidence that NVC is designed in such a way that the basic process of connecting with others—making clear observations, expressing and receiving feelings and needs, and making clear requests—remains effective no matter what social-change effort you apply it to.

ORIGINS OF NONVIOLENT COMMUNICATION

*"I object to violence because when it appears
to do good, the good is only temporary;
the evil it does is permanent."*

—MAHATMA GANDHI

I started looking at new forms of communication because of a couple of questions that had been in my mind since childhood. My family moved to Detroit, Michigan, just in time for the race riots of 1943. In our neighborhood thirty people were killed in about four days. We had to stay in the house those four days; we *couldn't* go out. This was a very powerful education for me as a boy. It was a painful education but one that brought to my awareness the idea that this is a world where people might want to hurt you because of the color of your skin.

What is it that gets into people that makes them want to harm people?

Then when I went to school for the first time, I found out that my last name could be a stimulus for people wanting to do violence to me. So it was on my mind repeatedly as a child growing up: What is it that gets into people that makes them want to harm people for such reasons as their name, their religion, their background, or their skin color?

Fortunately, I was also exposed to the other side of human beings. For example, my grandmother was totally paralyzed, and my mother was caring for her. And each evening an uncle of mine would come to our house to help my mother care for my grandmother. The whole time he was cleaning her up and feeding her, he had the most beautiful smile on his face.

So as a boy I kept wondering: How come there are people like my uncle who seem to enjoy contributing to the well-being of other people and at the same time other human beings who want to do violence to one another? When it came time to make decision about what kind of work I wanted to do, I thought I would like to study these pivotal questions.

Initially I chose clinical psychology to find out what I could about those two questions. I ended up with a doctorate, but there were some limits to what I was taught that didn't answer the questions as well as I would have liked. I was more interested in learning how we were meant to live and what moves people away from their violent tendencies. I studied on my own after graduate school to try to find out what I could about why people like my uncle enjoy contributing to the well-being of others and why other people seem to enjoy making others suffer.

> *Our nature:*
> *contributing to*
> *one another's*
> *well-being.*
>
>

I came to what I'll be sharing with you from a number of different directions. The main one was studying the people I really admired to see what made them different. Why did they enjoy contributing to people's well-being even when they were involved in or in the middle of conflicting situations in which people around them were behaving in a destructive way.

I talked to people like that, looked at them, and learned what I could from them about what they had learned. I looked at what helped them stay with what I really think is our nature: contributing to one another's well-being. I studied comparative religions to see if I could learn some things from the basic religious practices. These religions seemed to agree somewhat about how we are meant to live. Certain research—like that of Carl Rogers studying characteristics of healing relationships—was also very helpful to me.

From all of these sources I put together a process based on my desire for how I would like human beings to behave. If I can clarify for you the *purpose* of the process I was looking for, then it will make the mechanics of the process come more alive. That's because Nonviolent Communication is really an integration of a certain spirituality with concrete tools for manifesting this spirituality in our daily lives, our relationships, and our political activities. Therefore, I'd like to begin by clarifying the spiritual consciousness I was trying to serve by looking for the skills I'll be discussing later.

PURPOSE OF NVC

"Teach this triple truth to all: A generous heart,
kind speech, and a life of service and compassion
are the things which renew humanity."

— THE BUDDHA

The spirituality embodied in NVC exists not so much to help people connect with the divine as to come from the divine energy we're created out of, our natural life-serving energy. It's a living process to keep us connected to the life within our self and the life that's going on in other people.

Milton Rokeach, a research psychologist at Michigan State University, studied eight of the basic religions on the planet to see if, in any one of them, the people who seriously practiced the religion were more compassionate than others. He found that the eight he studied were about equal in compassion.

But then he compared them to people who had no religious affiliation—and the people with no religious affiliation were far more compassionate! He warned the reader, however, to be careful how one interprets these findings because within each religion there are two distinctly different populations. If you separated out a minority group (I think it was about twelve percent) from the majority, this small minority was far more compassionate than the non-churchgoing people.

For example, I was working in a village in Palestine and, at the end of a session, a young man said to me, "Marshall, I really liked your training, but you know, this is nothing new, and I don't mean this as a criticism: It's really just applied Islam."

He saw me smiling and said, "Why do you smile?"

I said, "Yesterday I was in Jerusalem, and an orthodox rabbi told me it was applied Judaism. And the head of our program in Sri Lanka is a Jesuit priest, and he thinks it's Christianity."

So the spirituality of that minority from each of the religions is very close to that which Nonviolent Communication is intending to serve.

NVC is a combination of thinking and language.

NVC is a combination of thinking and language, as well as a means of using power designed to serve a specific intention. This intention is to create the quality of connection with other people and oneself that allows compassionate giving to take place. In this sense it is a spiritual practice: All actions are taken for the sole purpose of willingly contributing to the well-being of others and ourselves.

The primary purpose of Nonviolent Communication is to connect with other people in a way that enables giving to take place: compassionate giving. It's compassionate in that our giving comes willingly from the heart. We are giving service to others and ourselves—not out of duty or obligation, not out of fear of punishment or hope for a reward, not out of guilt or shame, but for what I consider part of our nature. It's in our nature to enjoy giving to one another. Nonviolent Communication helps us connect with one another by allowing our nature to come forward in how we give (and are given to) by others.

When some people hear that I think it's our nature to enjoy giving, they wonder, I'm sure, whether I'm a little bit naïve and unaware of all the violence in the world. How can you think it's our nature to enjoy compassionate giving with what's happening in the world? Believe me, I see the violence. I work in places like Rwanda, Israel, Palestine, and Sri Lanka.

While I'm well aware of all the violence, I don't think that's our nature. In every place I work I ask people to think of something they've done within the last twenty-four hours that in some way has contributed to making life more wonderful for somebody. After they think a minute I ask, "Now, how do you feel when you are aware of how that act contributed to making life more wonderful for somebody?" And they all have a smile on their face. It's universal; most people enjoy giving to others.

Nothing is more enjoyable than using our efforts in the service of life.

When we are aware of the power we have to enrich life, how we can serve life, it feels good. I often follow up with the question, "Can anybody think of anything that's more fulfilling in life than to use our efforts this way?" I've asked this question all over our planet, and everyone seems to agree. There's nothing that is better, nothing that *feels* better, nothing that's more enjoyable than using our efforts in the service of life by contributing to one another's well-being.

Well, if that is so, then how come the violence? Well, I believe that *the violence comes because of how we were educated, not because of our nature.* I agree with the theologian Walter Wink, who believes that since the dawn of civilization—at least eight thousand years—we have been educated in a way that makes violence enjoyable. This kind of education gets us disconnected from our compassionate nature.

And why were we educated this way? That's a long story. I won't go into it here except to say that it started long ago with myths about human nature that framed humans as basically evil and selfish—and that the good life is heroic forces crushing evil forces. We've been living under this destructive mythology for a long time, and it comes complete with a language that dehumanizes people and turns them into objects.

We have learned to think in terms of moralistic judgments of one another. We have words in our consciousness like *right, wrong, good, bad, selfish, unselfish, terrorists, freedom fighters.* And connected to these judgments is a concept of justice based on what we "deserve." If you do bad things, you deserve to be punished. If you do good things, you deserve to be rewarded.

NVC brings us closer to our nature.

Unfortunately, we have been subjected to this consciousness, this faulty education, for a long, long time. I think that's the core of violence on our planet.

Nonviolent Communication, by contrast, is an integration of thought, language, and communication that I think brings us closer to our nature. It helps us to connect with one another so we come back to what is really the fun way to live, which is contributing to one another's well-being. As I show you how to apply this process within ourselves, our relationships, and in social-change efforts, I've provided exercises throughout the book to help you interact with the ideas you're learning—and even apply them as you go along.

For example, let's begin by having you think of a situation that's current in your life in which somebody is behaving in a way that isn't making life wonderful for you. This could range all the way from a minor irritation they created to something major that's bothering you about how this person behaves. But pick a real situation, and I'll show you how Nonviolent Communication can support you in creating a connection in that situation that will end with everybody's needs getting met, with the people involved acting solely for the purpose of enriching life for one another, which certainly includes meeting our own needs. Now, if you have the person in mind, we'll see how Nonviolent Communication serves us.

Wherever I do workshops around the world it seems like there's always one parent who has a two- or three-year-old they want to work on. And what is the behavior that this child does that drives them nuts? The child says horrible things like "No" when they want the child to do something.

"Please put your toys back in the toy box."

"No."

Some people tell me they live with partners who say

horrible things like, "That hurts me when you do that."

And some of the people I work with have much more serious issues, and they want to see how Nonviolent Communication can apply. In places like Rwanda, people might want to know, "How do I deal with my next-door neighbor when I know they killed a member of my family?"

EXERCISE:

If you would like to get a practical understanding of the Nonviolent Communication process, I suggest that you participate in the exercises placed throughout this book. Each exercise builds on the work you'll do in the previous one. To get the benefit of this experience, you can begin by thinking of an interaction with another person that hasn't gone in a way you enjoy and where you would like to learn how to speak peace.

Whatever circumstance you can recall at the moment, big or not so big, write it down or make a mental note of it: one specific thing that this person does that makes life less than wonderful for you. It could be something they do, something they don't do, or something they say or don't say. Now that you have noted something that this person does that you don't like, keep this in mind as you read the overview of how to apply Nonviolent Communication when you communicate with this person.

PART I

THE MECHANICS
OF SPEAKING PEACE

*"The most powerful agent of growth and
transformation is something much more basic
than any technique: a change of heart."*

— JOHN WELWOOD

CHAPTER 1

THE TWO QUESTIONS

"Don't ask yourself what the world needs.
Ask yourself what makes you come alive, and then
go and do that. Because what the world needs
is people who have come alive."

— HAROLD WHITMAN

NONVIOLENT COMMUNICATION KEEPS OUR ATTENTION focused on two critical questions.

Question number one: What's alive in us? (Related questions are: What's alive in me? What's alive in you?) Now, this is a question that all over the planet people ask themselves when they get together. They don't necessarily use those exact words. In English they often say it this way: How are you? Every language has its own way of asking, of course, but however it's said, it's a very important question.

We say it as a social ritual, but it's a very important question because, if we're to live in peace and harmony, if we're to enjoy contributing to each other's well-being, we

NVC shows us how to connect with what's alive.

need to know what's alive in each other. Sadly, though most people ask the question, not many people really know how to answer it very well because we haven't been educated in a language of life.

We've not really been taught to answer the question. We ask it, yes, but we don't know how to answer it. Nonviolent Communication, as we'll see, suggests how we can let people know what's alive in us. It shows us how to connect with what's alive in other people, even if they don't have words for saying it. So, that's the first question that Nonviolent Communication focuses our attention on.

The second question—and it's linked to the first—is: What can we do to make life more wonderful? (Related questions are: What can you do to make life more wonderful for me? What can I do to make life more wonderful for you?) So these two questions are the basis of Nonviolent Communication: What's alive in us? What can we do to make life more wonderful?

Now, just about everybody who studies Nonviolent Communication says two things about it. First, they say how easy it is, how simple. All we have to do is keep our communication, our focus of attention, our consciousness, on what's alive in us, what would make life more wonderful. How simple. The second thing they say is how difficult it is.

Now, how can something be so simple and so difficult at

the same time? Well, I've already given you a hint about that. It's difficult because we've been programmed to think and communicate in a quite different way. We haven't been taught to think about what's alive in us.

So, if we have been educated to fit under structures in which a few people dominate the many, we have been taught to think more of what people—especially authority figures—think of us. The reason is that if they judge us as bad, wrong, incompetent, stupid, lazy, or selfish, we're going to get punished. And if they label us as good little boys and girls, good students, and good employees, then we might be rewarded. We've been educated to think in terms of rewards and punishment instead of what's alive in us and what would make life more wonderful.

We've been educated to think in terms of rewards and punishment.

Let's go back to the situation I asked you to think about where somebody is behaving in a way you don't like. Let's look at how Nonviolent Communication suggests that we let that person know what's alive in us in relationship to what they're doing. We want to be honest in Nonviolent Communication, but we want to be honest without using words that imply wrongness, criticism, insult, judgment, or psychological diagnosis.

CHAPTER · 2

How Can We Express What's Alive in Us?

Observations

"You can observe a lot just by watching."

— Yogi Berra

To say what's alive in us requires specific kinds of literacy. First of all, it requires being able to give answers to the question I asked you without mixing in any evaluation. I asked you to think of one specific thing that a person did that you don't like. That's what I call an *observation*. What do people do that we either like or don't like?

That's important information to communicate: To tell people what's alive in us we need to be able to tell them what they're doing that is supporting life in us, as well as what they're doing that isn't supporting life in us. But it's very important to learn how to say that to people without mixing in any evaluation.

For example, I was working recently with a woman who was concerned about something her teenage daughter didn't do. So I said, "What was it that your teenage daughter didn't do?" And she said, "She's lazy." Can you hear a difference between the question I asked and the answer she gave? I asked what the daughter *does* and she told me what she thought the daughter *was*. I pointed out to this person that labeling people—diagnosing them as lazy—leads to self-fulfilling prophecies.

Any words we use that imply the wrongness of others are tragic, suicidal expressions of what's alive in us. They're tragic and suicidal because they don't lead to people enjoying contributing to our well-being. They provoke defensiveness and counter-aggression.

Diagnosing people leads to self-fulfilling prophecies.

When I first learned this lesson, it was very frightening to me because I saw how much my head was filled with moralistic judgments. I'd been taught throughout my education to think in terms of moralistic judgments. As I mentioned, the reason is this theory of human beings we have been inflicted with—that human beings are basically selfish and evil. Therefore, the prevailing educational process is one of making people hate themselves for what they've done. The idea is, you have to get them to see how terrible they are, and then they will be penitent and change the error of their ways!

The language I was educated to speak growing up in

Detroit was like that. When I was driving, if somebody else was driving in a way I didn't like and I wanted to educate them, I would open up the window and yell something like, "Idiot." The theory is they're supposed to feel guilty and repent, and they're supposed to say, "I'm sorry. I see that I was wrong. I've seen the error of my ways."

That's quite a theory, but it never worked. I thought maybe it was this particular dialect I learned in Detroit, but when I got my doctorate in psychology I learned how to insult people in a much more educated way. So now when I'm driving and somebody drives in a way I don't like, I roll down the window and yell something like, "Sociopath!" But it still doesn't work, you see.

Telling people what's wrong with them is suicidal and tragic—and besides, it's ineffective. We don't want these judgments to mix in when we try to tell people what they've done that we don't like. We want to go directly to the behavior without mixing in judgments. I was working with some teachers having a conflict with their administrator. I said, "What does he do that you don't like?"

One of them said, "He has a big mouth."

"No," I said, "I didn't ask you what size mouth he has. I asked you what he does."

Another one said, "Well, I know what he means. He talks too much."

I said, "*Too much* is another diagnosis, you see."

Another one said, "Well, he thinks he's the only one with any intelligence."

Get clear about defining behaviors without mixing in a diagnosis.

"Telling me what you think he thinks is an evaluation. What does he *do*?"

With my help they finally got clear about defining behaviors without mixing in a diagnosis, but along the way they kept saying, "Boy, this is hard to do. Everything that comes into our head is a diagnosis or judgment."

I said, "Yes, it isn't easy to get this cleared out of our consciousness." In fact the Indian philosopher Jiddu Krishnamurti says the highest form of human intelligence is the ability to observe without evaluating.

The teachers finally did come up with some behaviors. The first on the list was that during their staff meetings, no matter what was on the agenda, the administrator would relate it to one of his war experiences or childhood experiences. As a result the average meeting lasted longer than scheduled. OK, now that was the answer to my question of what he did. That was a clear observation that didn't mix in any evaluation.

I said to them, "Have any of you brought to his attention this specific behavior that concerns you?"

Then one of them said, "Well, we can see that the way we communicated it was in the form of a judgment, and we really didn't just mention the specific behavior. No wonder he got defensive."

So this is the first step in trying to tell people what's alive in us. It's the ability to call to their attention—concretely, specifically—what the person is doing that we like or don't like, without mixing in an evaluation.

EXERCISE:

Take a look at what you wrote down. See whether it had any evaluation mixed in. If so, see if you can now say it, being very specific, just describing what the person does that you want to talk to them about. Now that we have an observation in mind of what this person does, if we're to use Nonviolent Communication, we want to be honest with them about it. But it's honesty of a different kind than telling people what's wrong with them. It's honesty from the heart, not honesty that implies wrongness.

FEELINGS

"Our feelings are our most genuine
paths to knowledge."

— AUDRE LORDE

We want to go inside of ourselves and tell people what's alive in us when they do what they do. And this involves two other kinds of literacy. First, it involves *feeling literacy* and second, *need literacy*. To say clearly what's alive in us at any given moment we have to be clear about what we feel and what we need. Let's start with the feelings.

Let's imagine we go to this person and we want to be honest with them. Let's start by telling this person how we feel. Write down how you feel when the person does the behavior that you're thinking of. What emotions do you feel when they do it?

One student in the university I was working with wanted to work on his roommate. And I said, "OK, what is the behavior that your roommate does that you don't like?"

He said, "He plays the radio late at night when I'm trying to sleep."

"OK, so now let's tell him how you feel. How do you feel when he does that?"

He said, "I feel it's wrong."

I said, "I'm not making clear then what I mean by feelings. 'It's wrong' is what I would call a judgment of the other person. I'm asking you how you feel."

He said, "Well, I said 'I *feel*.'"

"Well, yeah, you used the verb *feel*, but that doesn't mean that what follows it is necessarily a feeling. What emotions do you feel? How do you feel?"

He thought for a while then said, "Well, I think that when a person is so insensitive to other people, it's evidence of a personality disturbance."

I said, "Hold it, hold it, hold it. You're still up in your head analyzing his wrongness. I'm asking, go into your heart, tell me how you feel when he does that."

He was sincerely trying to get in touch with his feelings, but he said, "Well, I don't have any feelings about it."

I said, "I hope that's not so."

He said, "Why?"

I said, "You'd be dead."

We have feelings every moment. The problem is we haven't been educated to be conscious of what's alive in us. Our consciousness has been more directed to make us look outward to what some authority thinks we are.

So I said, "Just listen to your body for a moment. How do you feel when he plays the radio that late at night?"

He really looked inside, and then he lit up and he said, "OK, I've got you now."

I said, "How do you feel?"

He said, "Pissed off."

"OK," I said, "that'll do. There are other ways of saying it, but OK."

But I noticed the woman sitting next to him, a faculty

> *It's important to
> have a vocabulary
> of feelings.*
>
>

member's wife, seemed a little perplexed. She looked at him and said, "Do you mean *vexed*?"

There are different ways we might express our feelings, depending on what culture we grow up in, but it's important to have a vocabulary of feelings that really does just describe what's alive in us and that in no way are interpretations of other people.

That means we don't want to use expressions like "I feel misunderstood." That's not really a feeling; it's more how we are analyzing whether the other person has understood us or not. If we think somebody has misunderstood us, we can be angry or frustrated; it could be many different things. Likewise, we don't want to use phrases like "I feel manipulated" or "I feel criticized."

In our training they're not what we would call feelings. Sadly, very few people have much of a feelings vocabulary, and I see the cost of that quite often in my work. If you'd like to see an extensive list of feelings, see the chapter on identifying and expressing feelings in my book *Nonviolent Communication: A Language of Life.*

It's rather typical for me to have a conversation like this: A woman in a workshop might come up to me and say, "You know, Marshall, I don't want you to get the wrong idea. I have a very wonderful husband ..."

I'm sure you can guess what the next word is. "*But* I never know how he's feeling."

I hear this a lot from people. I hear from people that they've lived with their parents for years and have never really known what their parents are feeling. How sad to live with people and not have this access to what's alive in them.

So, take a look at what you wrote. Is it really an expression of what's alive in you, of your feelings? Make sure it's not a diagnosis of others—or thoughts about what they are. Go into your heart. How do you feel when the other person does what they do?

> *The cause of our feelings is not other people's behavior.*
>
>

Feelings can be used in a destructive way if we try to imply that other people's behaviors are the cause of our feelings. The cause of our feelings is not other people's behavior, it's our needs. The observation you wrote down about what the other person did is a *stimulus* for your feelings, not the *cause* of your feelings. I'm sure most of us knew this at one time.

When I was six years old in my neighborhood and somebody would call us a name, we used to chant: "Sticks and stones can break my bones, but names can never hurt me." We were aware, then, that it's not what other people do that can hurt you; it's how you take it.

Unfortunately, we were educated in guilt-inducing ways by authorities—teachers, parents, etc.—who used guilt to mobilize us to do what they wanted. They might have expressed feelings this way:

"It hurts me when you don't clean up your room."

"You make me angry when you hit your brother."

We've been educated by people who tried to make us feel responsible for their feelings so we would feel guilty. Yes, feelings are important, but we don't want to use them in that way. We don't want to use them in a guilt-inducing manner. It's very important that when we do express our feelings we follow that expression with a statement that makes it clear that the cause of our feelings is our needs.

EXERCISE:

Write down the following in relation to what the other person has done. Identify how you feel about what happened and write it this way: "When you do what you do I feel _____." Put into words how you feel when the other person behaves as they do.

NEEDS

*"Understanding human needs is half
the job of meeting them."*

— ADLAI STEVENSON

Let's look at the third component of expressing what's alive in us: needs. Just as it's difficult for many people to observe without judgment and to develop a literacy of feelings, it's also very difficult for them to develop a literacy of needs. Many people associate needs with something negative. They associate needs with being needy, dependent, and selfish.

Again, I think that comes from our history of educating people to fit well into *domination structures* so they are obedient and submissive to authority. I'll talk more about domination structures later on, but for now just think of them as organized control over others. Most governments, schools, companies— and even many families—operate as domination structures.

> *People who are in touch with their needs do not make good slaves.*
>
>

The problem with people who are in touch with their needs is that they do not make good slaves. I went to schools for twenty-one years, and I can't recall ever being asked what my needs were. My education didn't focus on helping me be more alive, more in touch with myself and others. It was oriented toward rewarding me for giving right answers as defined by authorities.

Take a look at the words you were using to describe your needs. The main thing is to make sure we don't get needs mixed up with what we're going to talk about next.

In a workshop I was doing recently, a woman was upset with the way her daughter was not cleaning up her room. I said, "What needs do you have in this situation that aren't getting met?"

She said, "Well, it's obvious. I need her to clean up the room."

"No," I said, "That's going to come next. That's the request. I'm asking what needs you have."

And she couldn't come up with it. She didn't know how to look inside and see what her needs were. Again, she had a language for diagnosing what was wrong with the daughter, that the daughter was lazy. She could tell what she wanted the daughter to do, but she didn't know how to identify her own needs. And this is unfortunate because it's when people see the needs of another person it stimulates their enjoyment of giving—because we all can identify with needs. All humans have the same basic needs.

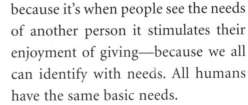

We see each other's humanness at the need level.

When we can connect at the need level, it's amazing how conflicts that seem unsolvable start to become solvable. We see each other's humanness at the need level. I do a lot of work with people in conflict. Husbands and wives, parents and children, tribes of people. Many of these people think they have a conflict that can't be resolved.

It's been amazing to me over the years of doing conflict resolution and mediation work what happens when you can get people over their diagnosis of each other, and get them to connect at the need level to what's going on in one another. When this happens, it seems as if conflicts almost resolve themselves.

At this point we have listed the three pieces of information that are necessary to say what's alive in us: what we're observing, what we're feeling, and the needs of ours that are connected to our feelings. (These are listed in the section at the back of this book titled *Some Basic Feelings and Needs We All Have.*)

EXERCISE:

Please write down the following in relation to what the other person has done and how you feel about it. Identify what needs are creating your feelings, and write it this way: "I feel as I do because I need ____." Put into words that need of yours that isn't being met by the other person's behavior.

CHAPTER · 3

HOW CAN WE MAKE
LIFE MORE WONDERFUL?

REQUESTS

*"Asking is the beginning of receiving. Make sure
you don't go to the ocean with a teaspoon. At least
take a bucket so the kids won't laugh at you."*

— JIM ROHN

NOW, LET'S TURN TO THE OTHER BASIC QUESTION: WHAT can be done to make life more wonderful? In the case of the person you've written about, you've recorded how you feel in relationship to their behavior. You've recorded what needs of yours aren't getting met. To respond to this second basic question of how to make life more wonderful, you're going to make a specific, clear request. You're going to request of the other person what you would like them to do to make life more wonderful for you.

Nonviolent Communication suggests that we make our

request using *positive action* language. Here's what I mean. Your language is positive in the sense that it requests what you *do want* the other person to do, rather than what you don't want or what you *want them to stop doing.* You want to request an action that involves them *doing* something. We get to a different place with people when we are clear about what we want, rather than just telling them what we don't want.

Make your request using positive action language.

∞

A teacher in a recent workshop provided a good example of that. She said, "Oh, Marshall, you've just helped me understand what happened to me yesterday."

I said, "What was that?"

She said, "There was this boy tapping on his book while I was talking to the class. So I said, 'Would you please stop tapping on your book?' So he started to tap on his desk."

You see, telling people what we don't want is far different from telling them what we do want.

When our objective is to get somebody to stop something, punishment looks like an effective strategy. But if we ask ourselves two questions, we would never use punishment again. We wouldn't use it with children, and we'd create a judicial system (a correctional system) that doesn't punish criminals for what they've done. We also wouldn't try to punish other nations for what they're doing to us. Punishment is a losing game. We will see that if we ask two questions.

Question number one: What do we want the other person to do? See, we're not asking what we don't want them to do. What do we want them to do? If we ask only that question, it can still make punishment seem like it

> *Punishment is a losing game.*
> ∞

works sometimes. We can probably recall times when we've used punishment and we were successful at getting somebody to do what we wanted them to do. But, if we add a second question, punishment never works.

And what is the second question? What do we want the other person's reasons to be for doing what we want them to do? As I've mentioned, the purpose of Nonviolent Communication is to create connections so people give to one another out of compassion—not out of fear of punishment, not out of hope for rewards, but because of the natural joy we feel of contributing to one another's well-being.

So, when we make our request, we want to do it in the positive, asking for what we do want. In the example I gave you earlier with the mother who wanted her daughter to clean up the room, I said, "Well, that wasn't the need, nor was it a clear request." So I said, "Let's first get the needs clear, and then we'll see how to make that request clearer. What need of yours is not met when your daughter has the room in the state it is?"

And the mother said, "Well, I think that if a family member is going to be a family member, each one has to contribute."

I said, "Wait a minute. Hold it, hold it. Saying what you think is a distorted expression of a need. If you want your daughter to see the beauty in your request, she needs to see how life will be made more wonderful if she does what you're asking. So, what is your need? What do you need that isn't being met?"

Develop your vocabulary of needs.

∞

The mother said, "I don't know."

And I wasn't surprised to hear that response because many women I work with have been educated from childhood to believe that loving women have no needs. They sacrifice their needs for their family.

Likewise, men have been taught that courageous men have no needs. They're even willing to sacrifice their life for the king, for the government, for whomever. So, we don't develop much of a vocabulary of needs. How can we make a clear request when we're not clear about our needs?

Finally, with my help, the mother did get clear what her needs were, and she had more than one need that was involved. First of all, the mother had a need for order and beauty. OK, she could have gotten that need met by herself, but the mother also had a need for some support, some help in creating the kind of order and beauty she would like. The mother then became conscious that two needs of hers were involved in this: her need for order and beauty, and her need for support in getting her needs met.

I said, "OK then, now let's get to your request. And let's

express it in positive action language. Say to your daughter what you *do* want."

She said, "Well, I told you. I want her to clean up the room."

"Not quite. We have to use action language. *Clean* is too vague. We have to use a concrete action to make our request."

So, what the mother finally came up with was that she would like the daughter to make the bed, to put clothes that were ready for the wash in the wash (and not leave them on the floor), and to take dishes back she had brought into her room back to the kitchen. That would be a clear request.

Now, once we have made this clear request, we need to make sure it's not heard as a demand. Earlier we talked about criticism—how anything that implies wrongness is a kind of communication that's not going to get our needs met. Another form of communication that's very destructive in human relationships is a *demand*.

EXERCISE:

Imagine that you've said the first three things to the person.

- *First, you've made an observation about what happened, without mixing in an evaluation.*

- *Second, you've expressed how you feel about what happened, free of blame and criticism.*

- *Third, you've expressed your needs in the situation, without referring to the other person or specific strategies.*

*Now write down what you would say to make a request. Put it this way: "I would like you to _____."
What would you like this person to do to make life more wonderful for you?*

REQUESTS VERSUS DEMANDS

"You've got to ask! Asking is, in my opinion,
the world's most powerful—and neglected—secret
to success and happiness."

— PERCY ROSS

We want to make clear, assertive requests, and we want other people to know that these are requests and not demands. What's the difference? First, you can't tell the difference by how nicely it is asked. So, if we do say to someone living with us, "I would like you to hang up your clothes when you're finished with them," is that a request or a demand?

We don't know yet. You can never tell whether something is a request or a demand by how nicely it is asked or how clear it is. What determines the difference between a request and a demand is how we treat people when they don't respond to our request. That's what tells people whether we make requests or demands.

What happens when people hear demands? Well, it's pretty obvious with some people when they've heard a request as a demand. One time I asked my youngest son, "Would you please hang up your coat in the closet?"

And he said, "Who was your slave before I was born?"

OK, it's fairly easy to be around such a person. If they hear your

> *What if people hear your request as a demand?*
>
>

request as a demand, you know it right away. But when other people hear a request as a demand, they respond quite differently. They'll say, "OK," but they don't do it. Or the worst case is when the person hears the demand and they say, "OK," and they do it. They did it because they heard a demand, and they were afraid of what would happen to them if they didn't.

Let me give you another example of what I mean by this demand thing. I was brought as a consultant into a hospital in New York City where they wanted the nurses to do certain critical sterilization procedures. In fact, the head nurse told me lives could be lost if these procedures were not followed: "Yet our research shows that a certain percentage of the time they're not being done. We've told them over and over they have to do it. We tell them it's unprofessional not to do it."

I already had a pretty good idea why it wasn't getting done. And I soon confirmed it because the next day I was to meet with the nurses. So I said to the nurses, "Yesterday it was brought to my attention that a certain percentage of the time these sterilization procedures are not being done. Are you aware of this?"

One of the nurses said, "Are we aware of it? We hear it every week."

"OK, then you know this is happening ..."

"Yes."

"Do you know the purpose of these procedures?"

"Of course. People could die if we don't do these sterilization procedures."

So they knew what was expected. They knew the

consequences. So the obvious question I asked next was, "Could you help me understand what keeps it from getting done?"

There was a reaction I get from everybody: silence. Finally a courageous nurse spoke up: "Uh, we forget."

You see, it's easy to forget things that you feel are imposed on you, things that are demanded of you. And when you don't do it, you get criticized. So it turned out that when I said, "You forget?" it opened up a discussion of the rage they felt for how this was being presented.

Make clear requests that people can trust as requests.

The more important the desired outcome is—when there are certain production standards or, in this case, preserving human life—the more important it is not to make demands. Make clear requests that people trust as requests. In order for them to trust that it's a request, they need to know that they can disagree and be understood.

So we have to show the managers, the head nurses, whomever, how to make clear requests, and then be able to empathize with dissent in a way that makes it safe for people to disagree. When you have that, you will come to agreements everybody will respect. That's one big thing we teach in the corporate world, in schools, and, of course, to parents.

Anytime somebody does what we ask out of guilt, shame, duty, obligation, or fear of punishment, we're going to pay for it. We want people to act on our request only when they're connected to a kind of divine energy that exists in all of us. This divine energy is manifest in the joy we feel in giving to one another. We're not doing it to avoid negative consequences. Now, some people don't believe you can have order in your home, business, organization, or government unless you make demands and force people to do things.

For example, another mother I worked with said, "But, Marshall, that's all well and good to hope that people are going to respond out of divine energy, but what about a child? I mean, a child has to first learn what they *have to* do, what they *should* do."

This well-intentioned mother was using two of the concepts that I think are the most destructive: *have to* and *should*. She didn't trust that there's divine energy in children, as well as in adults, that people can do things not because they're going to be punished if they don't, but because they see the joy that comes from contributing to other people's well-being.

Do things from the joy of contributing.

So I said to the mother, "I hope today I can show you other ways of presenting things to your children as more of a request. They see your needs. They don't do it because they think they have to. They see the choice and respond out of this divine energy within themselves."

She said, "I do all kinds of things every day that I hate to do, but there are just some things you have to do."

I said, "Could you give me an example?"

She said, "OK, here's one. When I leave here this evening, I have to go home and cook. I hate to cook. I hate it with a passion, but it's just one of those things I have to do. I've done it every day for twenty years. I hate it, but you have to do certain things."

Clearly, she wasn't doing that out of divine energy. She was doing that out of this other kind of consciousness. So I said to her, "I hope I can show you today a way of thinking and communicating that will help you get back in touch with your divine energy and make sure that you only come out of that. And then you can present things to others so they too can come out of that energy."

She was a fast learner. She went home that very night and announced to her family that she no longer wanted to cook. I got some feedback from her family. About three weeks later, who shows up at a training but her two older sons. They came up before the training, and one of them said to me, "We want to tell you how much change has occurred in our family since our mother came to your workshop."

I said, "Oh, yeah? You know, I've been very curious. She told me all the changes she's been making in her life since then, since she learned how to come out of a certain energy when she does things and doesn't do things because she thinks she has to. I always wonder how that affects other family members. So I'm glad you guys showed up tonight. For example, what was it like that first night when she came home and said she no longer wanted to cook?"

The oldest son said to me, "Marshall, I said to myself, 'Thank God.'"

Don't respond
unless you're
coming out
of divine
energy.

I said, "Help me to understand how you came to that."

He said, "I said to myself, *Now maybe she won't complain after every meal.*"

When we do things that don't come out of this divine energy in each of us, this divine energy that makes compassionate giving natural, when we come out of this culturally learned pattern of doing things because we *should/have to/must* to get rewards or out of guilt, shame, duty, or obligation … well, then everybody pays for it. Everybody.

Nonviolent Communication suggests we get clear: Don't respond unless it's coming out of this divine energy. And you'll know it is when you are willing to do it. Even if it's hard work, it will be joyful if your primary motive is to make life more wonderful.

Here's what happens if people hear demands instead of requests. When I was first learning Nonviolent Communication—initially getting all of this clear to myself—I had already started being a parent, but with old-school thoughts. So, I had to clean up messes for a while, because even when I was trying to be sure that when I made requests they were requests, it was still easy for my children to hear demands. You might recall that my youngest son said, in essence, that he felt like a slave when I asked him to do something.

In the days before I was using Nonviolent Communication,

that same son and I had a "garbage war" twice a week at our house. What was the garbage war? It was a war over this task I had given him. I said, "I want you to take over the job of taking out the garbage." This was a demand, because I believed that children should do tasks, so I wasn't telling him what need of mine would be met. I was telling him what he had to do, but putting it nicely. "This is your job; I would like you to take out the garbage." But because he was hearing it as a demand, we had the garbage war twice a week. And how did the garbage war start? Simply by my calling his name, "Brett!"

So, how does he fight the war? He's in the next room, and he pretends he doesn't hear me. Then I escalate the war even more. I yell now so loudly he can't pretend he doesn't hear me: "Brett!!"

"What do you want?"

"The garbage isn't out."

"You're very perceptive, Dad."

"Get it out."

"I'll do it later."

"You said that last time and didn't."

"Doesn't mean I won't do it this time."

Can you imagine so much energy going into just getting the garbage out twice a week? It happened twice a week, week after week, all because I was making a demand without realizing it. I didn't know the difference between a request and a demand at that time.

Later, as I was starting to learn Nonviolent Communication,

I sat with him one night and listened to why the garbage wasn't going out. And he made it clear that it was because he was hearing a demand.

It certainly helped me to get clear about the difference between requests and demands. For example, this was the same child who, when it snowed, would run down to the street corner to the home of a woman with a severe handicap. She couldn't walk, but she could drive her car. But when her driveway was filled with snow, she had no mobility. He would go down there and shovel her walk, and it would take him well over an hour to clear her driveway. He never told her who did it and never asked for money.

At our house, we had a tiny walkway to shovel. I couldn't get him to do it, and I wondered how come he would do all of this for the neighbor. It was obvious: For the neighbor it could come out of this divine energy that makes giving to others joyful. I was putting it to him in a domination structure: I'm the father, and I know what you have to do.

Be clear about the concept of "power over" versus "power with."

One final distinction we need to be clear about is the concept of "power over" versus "power with." Power over others gets things done by making people submit. You can punish, or you can reward. That's power *over*. It's very weak power because you have to pay for it. Research shows that companies, families, or schools that use power-over tactics pay for it indirectly through morale problems, violence, and subtle actions against the system.

Power *with* is getting people to do things willingly, because they see how it's going to enrich everybody's well-being by doing it. That's Nonviolent Communication. One of the most powerful ways we've found of creating power *with* people is the degree to which we show them we're just as interested in their needs as our own.

We create more power *with* people to the degree that we evaluate honestly and vulnerably without criticism. People are much more concerned about our well-being when we share power than when we tell them what's wrong with them.

EXERCISE:

*Look at your request of the person and the situation you recorded earlier. Is there a chance that your request will be perceived as power **over** them? What steps can you take to establish power **with** them and thereby increase the chance that they'll willingly respond to your request? How can you reword your request so that it reflects **positive action language?***

PART II

APPLYING NVC

*"The last of the human freedoms
is to choose one's attitudes."*

— VIKTOR FRANKL

AMERICA

Mexico

G. of
Mexico

L. Babba

OCEAN

Galapagos

Marque   Is

Low A

Tropic of Capricorn

Juan Fernand

OCEAN

Falkla

C. Horn   Tierra

S. Geo

ANTARCTIC OCEAN

CHAPTER · 4

CHANGE WITHIN OURSELVES

GROWTH THROUGH SELF-EDUCATION

*"Education is not a preparation for life;
education is life itself."*

— JOHN DEWEY

NOW I WOULD LIKE TO SHARE WITH YOU HOW NONVIOLENT
Communication can contribute to our attempts to
bring about change:

- within ourselves.
- in people whose behavior is not in harmony with
  our values.
- in the structures within which we're living.

Earlier I outlined that the purpose of Nonviolent
Communication is to create a connection that allows
compassionate giving to take place. And I clarified the basic
literacy that's necessary to live this way, which is a literacy of

feelings, needs, requests, and how to express them in a way that is a gift to other people so they can see what's alive in us.

It's a gift when they can see what would make life more wonderful because it gives them a chance to contribute willingly to our well-being. And I talked about how through empathic connection we can receive that gift from other people, even when they're using a language that is quite violent.

When we look at how Nonviolent Communication can contribute to change, remember this: We want people to change because they see better ways of meeting their needs at less cost, not because of fear that we're going to punish them, or "guilt" them if they don't. First, we'll look at how that change can occur within ourselves, then with other people whose behavior is not in harmony with our values, and then with social structures that are operating in ways that are not in harmony with our values.

First, ourselves: Think of a mistake you made recently, something you did that you wish you hadn't done. Then think, *How do I educate myself when I've done something I wish I hadn't done?* That is, what do you tell yourself at the moment you regret what you've done?

Learn from your limitations without losing self-respect.

Not long ago I was doing a training session, and we were seeing how Nonviolent Communication can be used within ourselves to learn from our limitations without losing self-respect. A woman told us she had been screaming at her child that morning before coming to the training. She said some things to the child that she wished she hadn't said—and when she looked into her child's eyes, she saw how hurt the child was. I asked her this question: "How did you educate yourself at that moment? What did you say to yourself?"

And she said, "I said *what a terrible mother I am*. I told myself that *I shouldn't have talked that way to my child*. I said, *What's wrong with me?*"

Unfortunately, that's how many people educate themselves. They educate themselves in a way people educated us when we did things that authorities didn't like. They blamed us and punished us, and we internalized it. As a result, we often educate ourselves through guilt, shame, and other forms of violent, coercive tactics. We know we're doing that. How do we know that we are educating ourselves in a violent way?

Three feelings will tell us: depression, guilt, and shame. I think we feel depressed a good deal of the time, not because we're ill or something is wrong with us, but because we have been taught to educate ourselves with moralistic judgments, to blame ourselves, to think like this mother did. She told herself that, because she had screamed at her child, there was something wrong with her, that she was a bad mother.

Incidentally, I often tell people, "If you want to know my definition of hell, it's having children and thinking there is such a thing as a good parent." You'll spend a good deal of your life being depressed, because it's a hard job. It's an important job, and repeatedly we're going to do things we wished we hadn't done. We need to learn, but without hating ourselves. Learning that occurs through guilt or shame is costly learning. It's too late now to undo that learning. We have it within ourselves. We've been trained to educate ourselves with violent judgments.

We show you in our training how to catch yourself when you're talking to yourself like that and to bring those judgments into the light, to see what you're telling yourself. You realize that this is your way of educating yourself—to call yourself names, to think of what's wrong with you. Then we show you how to look behind these judgments to the need at the root of them. That is to say, what need of yours wasn't met by the behavior?

> *Learn to look behind your judgments to the need at the root of them.*

And I asked this mother that very question: "What need of yours was not met by how you talked to the child?" With a little help from me, she got in touch with the need.

She said, "Marshall, I have a real need to respect people, especially my children. Talking to my child that way didn't meet my need for respect."

I said, "Now that your attention is on your needs, how do you feel?"

She said, "I'm sad."

I said, "How does that sadness feel compared with what

you were thinking a few moments ago—that you're a terrible mother and the other judgments you were making of yourself?"

She said, "It's almost like a sweet pain now."

"Yes, because it's a natural pain, you see."

When we get in touch with needs of ours that weren't met by our

Learn to mourn your actions without blame, without guilt.

behavior, I call that mourning—mourning our actions. But it's mourning without blame, mourning without thinking there's something wrong with us for doing what we did. When I help people get to that connection, they often describe the pain in a similar way to how she did. It's almost like a sweet pain compared with the depression, the guilt, and the shame we feel when we are educating ourselves through blame and judgments. I then asked her to look at the good reasons she did what she did.

She said, "Huh?"

I repeated my request: "Let's look at the good reasons you did what you did."

"I don't understand what you mean. You mean screaming at my child the way I did? What do you mean by *good reason*?"

I said, "It's important for us to be conscious that we don't do anything except for good reasons." I don't think any human being does anything except for good reasons. And what are those good reasons? To meet a need. *Everything* we do is in the service of needs.

So, I said, "What need were you trying to meet when you talked to your child that way?"

She said, "Are you saying it was right?"

"I'm not saying it was right to talk to the child that way. I'm suggesting that we learn to look at the needs we're trying to meet by doing what we do. We can learn best from it if we do two things. First, see the need that wasn't met by the behavior. And next, be conscious of the need we were trying to meet by doing what we did. When we have our awareness focused on those two needs, I believe it heightens our ability to learn from our limitations without losing self-respect."

"So, what need of yours were you trying to meet by saying what you did to the child at that time?"

She said, "Marshall, I really have a need for my child to be protected in life—and if this child doesn't learn how to do things differently, I'm really scared of what could happen."

"Yes. So you really have a need for your child's well-being, and you were trying to contribute …"

Be conscious of what need of yours was met by doing what you did.

She said, "That was a terrible way to do it—to scream like that."

"Well, we've already looked at that part of yourself that doesn't like what you did. It didn't meet your need to respect other people. Now let's be conscious of what need of yours was met by doing it. You care for the child; you wanted to protect the child's well-being."

"Yes."

"I believe we have a much better chance to learn how to handle other situations in the future if we ask ourselves how we could have met both needs. Now, when you have those two needs in mind, can you imagine how you might have expressed yourself differently?"

She said, "Yes, yes. Oh, yes. I can see that if I had been in touch with those needs, I would've expressed myself quite differently."

This is how we show people how to use Nonviolent Communication within themselves. When we do something we don't like, the first step is to mourn, to empathize with ourselves about the need of ours that wasn't met. And very often we'll have to do that by "hearing through" the judgments we have been programmed to make. In this way we can actually make good use of our depression, guilt, and shame. We can use those feelings as an alarm clock to wake us up to the fact that at this moment we really are not connected to life—life defined as being in touch with our needs. We're up in our head playing violent games with ourselves, calling ourselves names.

If we can learn how to empathically connect with the need of ours that wasn't met, and then look at the part of our self that was trying to meet the need, we're better prepared to see what's alive in ourselves and others—and to take the steps necessary to make life more wonderful.

Often it's not easy to empathically connect with that need. If we look inside and say what was going on in us when we did that, very often we say things to ourselves like "I had to do it; I had no choice." That's never true! We always have a choice. We don't do anything we didn't choose to do. We chose to behave that way to meet a need. A very important part of Nonviolent Communication is this recognition of choice at every moment, that every moment we choose to do what we do, and we don't do anything that isn't coming out of choice. What's more, every choice we make is in the service of a need. That's how Nonviolent Communication works within us.

SELF-EMPATHY FOR OUR 'MISTAKES'

"Let us be glad of the dignity of our privilege
to make mistakes, glad of the wisdom that
enables us to recognize them, glad of the power
that permits us to turn their light as a glowing
illumination along the pathway of our future.
Mistakes are the growing pains of wisdom.
Without them there would be no individual
growth, no progress, no conquest."

— WILLIAM JORDAN

Many people have a great deal of pain surrounding things they've done or experienced in their lives. In helping people address the source of their pain, the first thing we do is get them to be conscious of the things they're telling themselves about what creates their pain.

In this way, Nonviolent Communication is very much in harmony with the principles of psychiatrist Thomas Szasz, as expressed in his book *The Myth of Mental Illness*. Yes, there are some physical problems some people have that affect mental well-being, but the vast majority of people we call mentally ill are simply "well-educated" to think and communicate in a way that causes them great psychological discomfort. It doesn't mean they're ill; it means they've learned ways of thinking and communicating that make life pretty miserable.

So, our first step in helping people is to show them how to learn from their mistakes without losing self-respect. Or, as I say it in my Detroit way, how to enjoy mucking things up. We first have them learn by asking them to think of a mistake. That's why we exclude perfect people from our workshops, because we don't want people to come and having nothing to work on!

We start by asking people to think of something they have done that they didn't like doing. Then we ask them to give us a little snippet of how they spoke to themselves. You know, it's pretty brutal what people say to themselves—and not just on the golf course. The most common response, the number one comment of all time, is "You *idiot!*" I'll tell you right now, there are a lot of idiots in the world. Still others use a violent word, one of the most violent words human beings have ever developed: *should*. "I shouldn't have done that. I should have been more sensitive."

The word "should" creates enormous pain.

The word *should* comes directly from this game of violence that implies there's a good and a bad, a *should* and a *shouldn't*. If you don't do the things you should do, you should be punished; if you do the right things, you should be rewarded. This creates enormous pain. So we get people to identify what they say to themselves when they are less than perfect. And it brings back a lot of memories for people.

They can see that they're still telling themselves the things they used to hate their parents saying to them when they were young children. "You should have known better; you're careless; you're stupid; you're selfish; what's wrong with you?" They see now that they educate themselves the same way when they're less than perfect. And the first thing they do is call themselves some pretty brutal names. No wonder forty-one percent of pharmaceutical sales are for anti-depressants. Teach people to blame themselves when they've made mistakes, and you're going to have a lot of people spending a lot of their lives being depressed.

In helping people get past the pain of *should*, we start by helping them become conscious of this thinking. Then we show people that this thinking is all a tragic expression of an unmet need. It means that you didn't meet a need of yours by doing what you did, and if you can identify the need of yours that wasn't met, you're far more likely to learn from it because you'll start to imagine how you could have better met the need without losing self-respect. So, we get them to identify the brutal language they're using to blame themselves, and then we teach them how to translate such language into need language.

At this point we show people how to connect empathically with what was alive in them when they did the behavior that they called a mistake. In other words, get clear what need they were trying to meet by doing it. So rather typically a mother might say in a workshop, "I was running late and screamed at my children today in a way that I shouldn't have before I came to this training. I feel so guilty about it. I must be a terrible mother."

Connect empathically with what was alive in them.

"So, that's what you tell yourself about the screaming, that you think you're a terrible mother?"

"Yes."

And then we help her to get clear: "What needs of yours didn't get met, needs that are being expressed through these judgments that you're a terrible mother, that you shouldn't have behaved that way?"

"I want to be respectful to all people, but especially to my children."

"So, that is the need that wasn't met?"

"Yeah."

"Now how do you feel?"

"Oh, quite different. I feel sad, not so depressed, not so angry at myself."

"OK. Now, what need of yours were you trying to meet by doing it?"

"Oh, there was no excuse for it."

"No, there was in fact very good excuse for it. You were

doing it for the same reason all human beings do everything: to meet a need the best way you knew at that moment. What was your need?"

"Well, I wanted to respect you and the other members of this group by being on time."

We helped her to get clear about the desperation she was feeling from having this other need to be respectful of the time agreements we made. What we find is that when people can empathize with themselves in these ways ... then if they do start to criticize themselves, they know how to translate that criticism into an unmet need. When people can practice self-empathy, they are much better able to learn from their limitations without losing self-respect—without feeling guilty or depressed.

In fact, I would say that if we're not able to empathize with ourselves, it's going to be very hard to do it with other people. If we still think when we make a mistake that there's something wrong with us, then how are we not going to think there's something wrong with other people for doing what they do? When we can empathize with ourselves and really stay connected to our true self in a life-enriching way, we can hear or sense which needs we're not meeting by our actions, at which point we also can see which needs we were trying to meet by doing what we just did. When our awareness is on our needs, we're much better able to meet our needs without losing self-respect, and we're also better able to avoid judging others for what they say or do.

NVC helps us learn how to create peace within ourselves

when there's a conflict between what we do and what we wish we had done. If we're going to be violent to our self, how are we going to contribute to creating a world of peace? Peace begins within us. I'm not saying we have to get totally liberated from all of our inner, violent learning before we look outside of our self to the world,

> *NVC helps us learn how to create peace within ourselves.*
>
> ∞

or to see how we can contribute to social change at a broader level. I'm saying we need to do these simultaneously.

HEALING OLD HURTS—MOURNING VERSUS APOLOGY

"He that lacks time to mourn, lacks time to mend."

— SIR HENRY TAYLOR

Very often, a lot of healing work goes on in our trainings. Realize first of all that this takes place in front of as many as eighty or ninety people, so you might say there are many witnesses to the efficacy of our approach. Participants regularly tell me they get more out of thirty or forty minutes of what I've done than they received from six or seven years of traditional psychotherapy.

First of all, we talk very little if at all about what happened in the past. I have found that talking about what happened in the past not only doesn't help healing, it often perpetuates and increases pain. It's like reliving the pain. This goes very much against what I was taught in my training in psychoanalysis, but I've learned over the years that you heal by talking about what's going on in the moment, in the now.

> *You heal by talking about what's going on in the moment, in the now.*

Certainly it's stimulated by the past, and we don't deny how the past is affecting the present, but we don't "dwell" on it.

How do I do this? I often play the role of the person who stimulated most of the other person's pain in the past. Not infrequently this is a parent.

I might be playing the role of a father who beat or sexually molested this person as a child. So now I'm sitting with this person who's been in pain for years about this, and I play the role of the person who is the stimulus for the pain as though that individual knows Nonviolent Communication. I begin with empathy and say, "What's still alive in you as a result of what I have done?" See, we're not going into the past and talking about what I did, but about what's alive in you now that's still there from what happened in the past.

Often the person doesn't know Nonviolent Communication, so they don't know how to tell me what's alive in them except through diagnosis: "How could you do it? You know, you were cruel. How could a father beat a child that way?" And I start by saying, "So I'm hearing you say

_____," then I translate that into what they're feeling and needing, using Nonviolent Communication. Role-playing the father, I empathically connect with their pain, even if they're not expressing it in a very clear way.

In Nonviolent Communication we know that all these diagnoses are just tragic expressions of what a person is feeling and needing at this moment. So I continue until they have been fully understood about what's alive in them now that's still so painful. And then when they have received all the understanding they need, I mourn—still in the role of the father. Not apologize, but mourn.

Nonviolent Communication shows us a big difference between mourning and apology. Apology is basically part of our violent language. It implies wrongness—that you should be blamed, that you should be penitent, that you're a terrible person for what you did—and when you agree that you are a horrible person and when you have become sufficiently penitent, you can be forgiven. *Sorry* is part of that game. If you hate yourself enough, you can be forgiven, you see.

Apology is part of our violent language.

Now, in contrast, what is really healing for people is not that game where we agree that we're terrible, but rather going inside yourself and seeing what need of yours was not met by the behavior. And when you are in touch with that, you feel a different kind of suffering. You feel a natural suffering, a kind of suffering that leads to learning and healing, not to hatred of oneself, not to guilt.

So, in the role of the father, having empathized with my daughter, I then mourn. I might say something like, "I feel terribly sad to see that my way of handling my pain at the time could result stimulate so much pain for you. And my needs were not met by that. My needs were just the opposite, to contribute to your well-being." That might be what the mourning sounds like.

After the mourning, the next step is for the father to explain to the daughter what was alive in him when he did those horrible things in the past. We do go into the past at this point, not to talk about what happened but to help the daughter see what was alive in the father at the time he did this.

In some cases the father might sound like this: "I was in such pain in so many parts of my life—my work wasn't going well, I was feeling like a failure—so when I would see you and your brother screaming, I didn't know what else to do to handle my pain except in the brutal way that I did." When the father can honestly express what was alive in him, and the daughter can empathize with that, can see that, it's amazing how much healing can take place. What's surprising for some people is that all of this can happen in an hour—and in front of a room full of people.

EXERCISE:

Think of a person or event from the past that still brings you pain. What's alive in you at this moment about that person or event? What may have been alive in the others involved?

CHAPTER · 5

CONNECTING WITH OTHERS EMPATHICALLY

*"Man did not weave the web of life, he
is merely a strand in it. Whatever he does to
the web, he does to himself. All things are
bound together. All things connect."*

— CHIEF SEATTLE

WE'VE NOW LOOKED AT HOW WE EXPRESS WHAT'S ALIVE in us and what would make life more wonderful. We see how it requires observations, feelings, needs, and clear requests. But those are the mechanics. It's always important to realize that these mechanics have power only when they're used in the service of the spiritual purpose of the process, which is to create a connection so people can respond out of divine energy, the joy of compassion, the joy of giving. If we do not have that intentionality, we've missed the whole thing.

For example, one mother came back on the second day of a workshop and said, "I went home and tried it last night, Marshall, and it didn't work."

I said, "Well, let's learn from the experience. What did you do?"

She told me how she expressed herself to one of her children who hadn't done something she wanted. And she used the mechanics perfectly. She made a very clear observation, expressed her feelings, needs, and requests. But he still didn't do it.

I said, "So, what do you mean it didn't work?"

"Well," she said, "he didn't do it."

"Oh, so you're defining it as not working because he didn't do what you wanted him to do?"

"Yes."

"Well, that's not Nonviolent Communication; even if you used the mechanics, that's not the idea. Remember yesterday I said the purpose is to create a quality of connection that allows us to give to one another out of the joy of compassionate giving. It's not just to get what you want."

"Oh," she said, "so I'm just supposed to do all the work around the house myself …?"

She made the mistake that many people make by thinking that if we don't get people to do what we want, the only other option is to give up and be permissive, to have anarchy. And I showed her if we connect in the way I'm talking about, everybody's needs can get met. But if the other person senses that we have single-mindedness of purpose to get our request complied with, it changes the game. Then it turns our requests into demands.

RESPONDING TO THE MESSAGES OF OTHERS

"We cannot live only for ourselves. A thousand
fibers connect us with our fellow-men; and along
those fibers, as sympathetic threads, our actions
run as causes, and they come back to us as effects."

— HERMAN MELVILLE

Let's consider a situation in which you've been honest with another person as defined in Nonviolent Communication terms. That's half the process: learning how to express ourselves in this way. The other half of the process is how we respond to other people's messages.

Let me tell you what many people are afraid will happen if they open up and reveal themselves. When they reveal honestly what's alive in them and what would make life more wonderful, many people are afraid they're going to get a free diagnosis from the other person. The other person is going to tell them what's wrong with them for having these feelings, needs, and requests. They're afraid they'll hear things about how they're too sensitive, needy, or demanding. This can happen, of course. We live in a world where people think that way, so if we are really open and honest, we might get back a diagnosis. Good news, though! Nonviolent Communication prepares us to deal with any response that might come back.

Many other
people are afraid
of a tiny two-
letter word: No.

Other people are afraid of silence. They say, "What if I open up and reveal myself and the other person doesn't say anything?" We can prepare for that too. Many other people are afraid of a tiny two-letter word: No. They say, "What if I open up and say what I want and need and the other person says no." Look at what you wrote down. We want to prepare for anything that can come back at us.

The other half of Nonviolent Communication shows us how to make empathic connection with *what's alive in the other person* and *what would make life more wonderful for them.* Empathic connection has a very specific meaning and purpose. Empathy, of course, is a special kind of understanding. It's not an understanding of the head where we just mentally understand what another person says. It's something far deeper and more precious than that.

Empathic connection is an understanding of the heart in which we see the beauty in the other person, the divine energy in the other person, the life that's alive in them. We connect with it. The goal isn't intellectually understanding it, the goal is empathically connecting with it. It doesn't mean we have to feel the same feelings as the other person. That's sympathy, when we feel sad that another person is upset. It doesn't mean we have to have the same feelings; it means we are *with* the other person. This quality of understanding requires one of the most precious gifts one human being can give to another: our presence in the moment.

> *If you're mentally trying to understand the other person, you're not present with them.*
>
>

You see, if we're mentally trying to understand the other person, we're not present with them in this moment. We're sitting there analyzing them, but we're not *with* them. Empathic connection involves connecting with what is alive in the other person *at this moment*. Look again at your prediction of how the other person might respond.

Let's say that you have told your boss you are frustrated at his or her asking you to stay over for the third night in a row and do additional work. You're frustrated because you have other commitments and needs that you'd like to take care of. So, you've been honest about your reasons for not wanting to do the overtime, and you ended on a clear request, like asking him if he would be willing to find someone else to help with the work this evening.

You've been honest and vulnerable, but now let's imagine that the boss says to you, "If you want to be unemployed, I'll do as you ask." What choices do you have now? Let me show you what choices you have with every message coming at you from another person.

Choice number one: You can take it personally, as though what you requested indicated there was something wrong with you. So, if the boss responds to you that way, you could immediately think, *I am being selfish* or *I'm not a very good employee.* You could take what the boss says personally.

We have been educated that when authorities tell us what's wrong, we think there is something wrong with us. I suggest that you never, never, never listen to what other people think about you. I predict you'll live longer and enjoy

> *Learn to connect empathically with any message coming at us from other people.*
>
>

life more if you never hear what people think about you. And never take it personally.

The second choice we have when somebody speaks to us like the boss spoke is to judge the boss or the other person for what they said to us. We could either think or say aloud, *That's not fair*, *That's stupid*, or whatever. We could blame the other person for what they said. I wouldn't recommend that. The recommendation I have is to learn to connect empathically with any message coming at us from other people. To do that you have to see what's alive in them.

I've been quoted on the subject of empathy in a recent book edited by Josh Baran titled *365 Nirvana Here and Now: Living Every Moment in Enlightenment*. The author excerpts a passage in which I compared empathy to surfing. I said that empathy is like riding on a wave; it's about getting in touch with a certain energy. But the energy is a divine energy that's alive in every person, at every moment.

Unfortunately, many of us are blocked from that divine energy by the way we've been taught to think. But for me empathy is getting with that energy that's coming through the other person. It's a divine experience. I feel as if I'm really in a flow with divine energy. And when two people connect in that way, any kind of conflict can be resolved so that everybody's needs get met.

When we teach people to empathize with people from

other cultures who are behaving in ways we don't like, we find ways of resolving our differences peacefully. So empathy is a beautiful experience when we have it. And it's powerful to work toward peace in diplomatic relationships based on empathy, not on our usual adversarial tactics.

Now, when we can empathize with what's alive in another person, it's amazing how much healing can go on. Unfortunately, there's a lot of healing that needs to happen in the world because of the pain people are in, and I'm often called to help individuals who have been victimized by people with different religious beliefs.

Unfortunately, there's a lot of healing that needs to happen in the world.

For example, I did some healing work with a woman from Algeria who had been dragged outside by people who didn't like how she and her friend were dressing. She was forced to watch while they tied her friend behind a car and dragged her to her death. Then they took this woman into the house and raped her in front of her parents. The people were going to come back the next night and kill her, but fortunately she got to a phone and called some colleagues of mine in Geneva, Switzerland, who are skilled at getting people out of difficult situations.

They got her out, called me up, and said, "Marshall, could you see this woman for some healing work? She's in terrible pain. She's been in Switzerland now two weeks, crying day and night."

I said, "OK, send her out this evening. I'd be glad to do the work with her."

They said, "One thing you need to know, Marshall: She's afraid she'll kill you."

I said, "You explained that I will play the role of the person, but that I'm not the other person?"

"Yes, she understands that. But she said that if she even imagines you as the other person, she might hurt you. And Marshall, you should know this about this woman: She's a rather large woman."

I said, "Thank you for the warning." Because she would be speaking a different language than I speak, I said, "Well, tell her I'll have my interpreter. He's a man from Rwanda who's in the training I'll be doing in the afternoon and, after the violence he's been exposed to, I don't think this will scare him. See if she'd feel safe doing the work with the two of us in the room."

So I met with her and played the role of the religious extremist who had done these things to her because he didn't like the way she and her friend were dressing and behaving. This took quite awhile. For about an hour and a half she screamed at me the pain she felt. I empathized in the Nonviolent Communication way, just hearing the deep pain in her at this moment. And then she screamed at me, "How could you do it?"

And I said, "I'd like to tell you what was going on in me when I did, but I first want to tell you how horrible I feel when I now see your pain." I mourned first, then I told her what was alive in me that caused me to do what I did. Then she got startled and said, "How did you know?"

I asked, "What do you mean?"

She said, "That's almost exactly what he said. How did you know?"

"The reason I knew is that I am that man, and so are you, and so are we all."

At the core of our humanity, we all have the same needs. So when I do this healing work, I don't go up into my head and think what's going on with this other person. Rather, I put myself in that role and say what would have been going on in me were I to do something like that. When she could hear that, it was amazing the healing that went on for her after all she'd been through. I've been in touch with her for nearly eight years now, and I know that the healing has sustained itself.

EXERCISE:

To prepare us to see how Nonviolent Communication suggests responding to other people, let's go back to your situation and use your imagination. Imagine you will try out what we've learned so far. You decide to go to this person and be honest with them, using the four steps to answer the two questions. You tell the other person the four things I've asked you to write down: what they've done that you don't like, how you feel, what needs of yours aren't met, and what your request is. Now, predict how they might respond and write that down.

CHAPTER 6

SEEING THE BEAUTY IN OTHERS

"Love is but the discovery of ourselves in others,
and the delight in the recognition."

— ALEXANDER SMITH

NONVIOLENT COMMUNICATION SHOWS US A WAY OF finding out what's alive in other people. It also shows us a way of seeing the beauty in the other person at any given moment, regardless of their behavior or language. You've seen that it requires connecting with the other person's feelings and needs at this moment. That's what's alive in them. And when we do it, we're going to hear the other person singing a very beautiful song.

I was working with some twelve-year-olds in a school in the state of Washington, showing them how to make empathic connections with people. They wanted me to show them how they could deal with parents and teachers. They were afraid of what they would get back if they opened up and revealed what was alive in them. One of the students said, "For example, Marshall, I was honest with one of my teachers. I said I didn't understand, and I asked her, 'Would you explain it again?' and the teacher said, 'Don't you listen? I've explained it twice already.'"

Another young man said, "Yesterday I asked my dad for something. I tried to tell him my needs, but he said, 'You're the most selfish child in the family.'"

So, these young people were eager to have me show them how to empathically connect with the people in their lives who use language like that. They only knew how to take it personally, to think there was something wrong with them. I showed the students that if you learn how to connect empathically with other people, you will hear that they are *always* singing a beautiful song. They are asking you to see the beautiful needs that are alive in them. I showed them that this is what you will hear behind every message coming at you from another human being if you connect to the divine energy in that person at that moment.

> *Learn how to connect empathically and you will hear they are* always *singing a beautiful song.*

Another example of this comes from a time when I was working in a refugee camp in a country not very pleased with the United States. There were about one hundred and seventy people assembled, and when my interpreter announced that I was an American citizen, one of them jumped up and screamed at me, "Murderer!"

Another one jumped up and shouted: "Child killer!"

Another: "Assassin!"

I was glad I knew Nonviolent Communication that day. It enabled me to see the beauty behind their messages, to see what was alive in them.

We do that in Nonviolent Communication by hearing feelings and needs behind any message. So I said to the first gentleman, "Are you feeling angry because your need for support isn't getting met by my country?"

Now, that required me to try to sense what he was feeling and needing. I could have been wrong. But even if we're wrong, if we are sincerely trying to connect with the divine energy in another human being—their feelings, their needs at that moment—that shows the other person that no matter how they communicate with us, we care about what's alive in them. When a person trusts that, we're well on our way to making a connection in which everybody's needs can get met.

Try to connect in a way that shows the other person you care about what's alive in them.

It didn't happen right away because this man was in a lot of pain. And it happened that I guessed right, because when I said, "Are you angry because your need for support isn't being met by my country?" he said, "You're #!@&%! right," adding: "We don't have sewage systems. We don't have housing. Why are you sending your weapons?"

I said, "So, sir, if I'm hearing you again, you're saying that it's very painful when you need things like sewage systems and housing—and when weapons are sent instead it's very painful."

He said, "You're #!@&%! right. Do you know what it's like to live under these conditions for twenty-eight years?"

"So, sir, you're saying that it's very painful, and you need some understanding for the conditions that you're living under." So I heard what was alive in the guy, not that he thought I was a murderer. When he trusted that I sincerely cared about what he was feeling, what he was needing, he could start to hear me.

Then I said, "Look, I'm frustrated right now because I came a long way to be here. I want to offer something, and I'm worried now that because you've got me labeled as an American, you aren't going to listen to me."

He said, "What do you want to say to us?"

So he could hear me then.

But I had to see the human being behind the names he was calling me. An hour later the gentleman invited me to a Ramadan dinner at his house. Incidentally, we now have a school in that refugee camp. We call it a Nonviolent Communication school. And whenever I go to that region I'm received hospitably in that camp.

This is what happens when we can connect with the humanness in each other, with the feelings and needs behind any message. This doesn't mean that we always have to say it out loud. Sometimes it's pretty obvious what the person is feeling and needing, and we don't have to say it. They'll feel from our eyes whether we're really trying to just connect with them.

Notice this doesn't require that we agree with the other person. It doesn't mean we have to like what they're saying. It means that we give them this precious gift of our presence, to be present at this moment to what's alive

> *They'll feel from our eyes whether we're really trying to connect with them.*

in them, that we are interested, sincerely interested in that. We don't do it as a psychological technique but because we want to connect with the beauty in the person at this moment.

Now, when we put this all together, it looks like this: We may start a dialogue with the other person by telling them what's alive in us and what we would like them to do to make life more wonderful for us. Then, no matter how they respond, we try to connect with what's alive in them and what would make life more wonderful for them. And we keep this flow of communication going until we find strategies to meet everybody's need.

> *No matter how people respond, try to connect with what's alive in them.*

We always want to be sure that whatever strategies people agree to, they're agreeing out of a desire to contribute to the well-being of one another and not out of the reasons I've outlined that we want to avoid—

like submitting to punishment, guilt, etc. Many people believe that you cannot do this with some people. They believe that some people are so damaged that, no matter what communication you use, you're not going to arrive at this point. That has not been my experience.

I'm not saying that this connection always happens right away. For example, with some prisoners I have worked with throughout the world, it may take quite awhile for some of them to really trust that I'm sincerely interested in what's alive in them. Sometimes it's not easy to stay with that because my own cultural conditioning hasn't allowed me to be fluent in this from an early age, and learning this can be a real challenge.

I recall one time when I was first learning NVC, my older son and I were having a conflict. My first reaction to what he was saying was not to connect with what was alive in him, with what he was feeling and needing. I wanted to jump in and show him he was wrong. I had to take a deep, deep breath. I needed to see what was going on in me for a moment and see that I was losing connection with him, then bring my attention back to him, saying, "So, you're feeling …" and "you're needing …" to try to connect with him.

Then he said something else, and again I got triggered and had to slow down and take a deep breath to be able to keep coming back to what was alive in him. Of course, all this was taking longer than usual in the conversation up to that point, and he had some friends waiting for him outside.

Finally, he said, "Daddy, it's taking you so long to talk."

I said, "Let me tell you what I can say quickly. Do it my way, or I'll kick your butt."

He said, "Take your time, Dad, take your time."

So, Nonviolent Communication requires that we take our time to come from our divine energy rather than our cultural programming.

> *Take your time.*
>
> ∞

CHAPTER · 7

WHAT DO YOU WANT
TO CHANGE?

"Progress is impossible without change,
and those who cannot change their minds
cannot change anything."

— GEORGE BERNARD SHAW

IF WE'RE GOING TO BE EFFECTIVE IN OUR EFFORTS TOWARD social change, it helps to be conscious of the work we need to do within our self. And while we're doing that, we also need to look outside of our self to the changes we would like to see happen in our world. Let's look at some of these changes and how Nonviolent Communication can help us.

Some people obviously behave in ways that are pretty frightening to us. People we call criminals ... they steal, they rape. What do we do if we're around people who behave in ways that we find repugnant, even frightening? How do we change these individuals or get them to change? Here's where we really need to learn to apply *restorative* justice. We need to learn not to punish people when they behave in ways we don't like.

As I've said earlier, punishment is a losing game. We want people to change behavior, not because they're going to be punished if they continue, but because they see other options that better meet their needs at less cost.

I tried to make this point clear to a mother in Switzerland at a workshop of mine. She said, "Marshall, how do I get my son to stop smoking?"

I said, "Is that your objective, to get him to stop smoking?"

She said, "Yes."

I said, "Then he'll continue."

She said, "Huh? What do you mean?"

Whenever our objective is to get somebody to stop doing something, we lose power.

I said, "Whenever our objective is to get somebody to stop doing something, we lose power. If we really want to have power in creating change—whether it's personal change, changing another individual, or changing society—we need to come from a consciousness of how the world can be better. We want people to see how their needs can better be met at less cost."

We then looked at how this would apply to her situation with her child. She was in great pain about this because she was worried about his health. He had been smoking for two years, and they had fights about it almost daily. Her objective was to get him to stop, and she was trying to accomplish this by telling him how horrible it was. She said, "Marshall, how would Nonviolent Communication help me in this situation?"

I said, "Well, I hope we've got the first part clear. Your objective is not to get him to stop. It's to *help him find other ways of meeting whatever needs the smoking is meeting at less cost.*"

She said, "That's helpful; that's really helpful. But how do I communicate that with him?"

I said, "Well, I would suggest starting by sincerely communicating to him that you see that his smoking as the most wonderful thing he could be doing."

She said, "Huh? What do you mean?"

I said, "He wouldn't be smoking if it wasn't meeting his needs. So if we can sincerely show an empathic

> *When people think we have single-mindedness of purpose, it makes change difficult.*

connection with what needs he's trying to meet, he'll see that we understand why he's doing it. We're not judging him or blaming him for it. When people feel that quality of understanding, then they're much more open to hearing other options. If they think we have single-mindedness of purpose to change them, or if they feel they're being blamed for what they're doing, it makes change difficult. So, the first step is to sincerely communicate that you see that what he's doing as absolutely the most wonderful way he knows to meet his needs."

This woman came back after lunch and she was glowing, just glowing. She said, "Marshall, thank you so much for what you've taught me this morning. I had the most wonderful communication with my son over lunchtime. I called him up on the phone."

I said, "Well, tell me about it."

The woman said, "First of all, when I called home, his thirteen-year-old brother answered. I said, 'Quick, put your brother on the phone. I want to talk to him.'

And my thirteen-year-old said, 'Uh, well, uh, he's on the back porch.' Then I knew he was smoking, because after two years of fighting about the smoking, at least he agreed that if he would smoke he would do it outside and not inside.

So I said to my thirteen-year-old son, 'That's OK. Just tell him I want to talk to him.'"

So, then the fifteen-year-old came on the phone and said, "What do you want?" And the mother said, "I learned something about your smoking today that I wanted to talk to you about."

"Well, what?"

She said, "I've learned that it's the most wonderful thing you could be doing."

Now I said to the mother, "That wasn't exactly how I meant for you to do that. I was really meaning that we communicate through empathic connection, showing that you understand."

She said, "Oh, oh, I got that, Marshall. I understood that. But, you know, I know this guy, and I really felt I could get that across to him much quicker by just stating that I see that smoking is the most wonderful thing he could be doing."

"Well," I said, "you know him, OK. So, what happened?"

She said, "Marshall, what happened was profound, especially if you know how much we had fought about this. First he was silent for a long time, then he said, 'I'm not so sure about that.'"

You see, once people don't have to defend themselves against our single-mindedness of purpose to change them, once they feel understood for what they're doing, it's much easier for them to be open to other possibilities.

> *When people feel understood, it's easier for them to be open to other possibilities.*

For example, when I'm working in prisons I use this same principle. If somebody is doing something I don't like, I try to begin with empathic connection with the needs they're trying to meet by doing what they're doing and, once I've understood that, I suggest looking for other ways of meeting their needs that are more effective and less costly.

I was invited into a prison in the state of Washington in the United States and was working with a young man who was in prison for the third time for sexually molesting children. I wanted to start by empathically connecting to what was alive in him when he was doing this to children. So I suggested that I would like to understand better what was going on in him when he did it—and asked what needs he was trying to meet by doing this. He looked stunned when I asked him that question.

He said, "What are you asking for?"

I said, "I'm sure you do it for a good reason. This is your third time in prison for this offense. I don't have to tell you that it's not a fun life for sex offenders in prison."

Find other ways of meeting your needs more effectively and at less cost.

"You're #!&$%! right it isn't."

"Yeah. So, obviously, if you are going to do this and have to pay so much for it, it must be meeting some needs of yours. Let's identify those needs, because I believe that once we understand those needs, we'll be able to find another way of meeting the needs more effectively and at less cost. So, what are your needs?"

He asked, "Are you saying it was right to do what I did?"

"No," I said, "I'm not saying it was right. I'm saying you did it for the same reason I do everything I do, to meet needs. So what needs are you meeting by doing this?"

He said, "I do it because I'm dirt."

"No, now you're thinking of what you are. How long have you thought you were dirt?"

He said, "My whole life."

I said, "Has it stopped you from doing this?"

"No."

"So, I don't think judging yourself is going to meet your

needs or the needs of people in your community. But I think everybody's needs can get met if we start by understanding what needs of yours are being met by doing that."

We aren't trained to think of what our needs are.

Obviously, he required some help on my part because he wasn't trained to think of what his needs were. He had been in prisons, schools, and a family that had made him feel like dirt. He had been educated to think of what he was, not what his needs were. We found many needs. Let me just give you a couple of them as examples of what goes on inside a person.

First, he took these children into his apartment and treated them very well. He showed them television programs they liked and gave them food they liked. I said, "What need of yours is met when you do that?" It turned out that this man had always been very lonely. He had never had his need met for community, for connection, for companionship. This was the best way he'd ever found to meet that need: bring these children in, treat them well. Of course, he could have met that need without sexually molesting them.

Then we turned to the molestation: "What need of yours was being met by that?" It took a while to get to it, because it wasn't easy for him to look inside and see. He realized that his need for doing that was for understanding, for empathy.

From the terror in their eyes, he felt that his victims understood what he felt when he was a child and his father had done this to him. He didn't realize that was his need. He

didn't know other ways of meeting that need. Once we got it
clear, it was obvious there were many other ways to meet that
need other than terrorizing children.

That's how we use Nonviolent Communication with
people who are behaving in ways we don't like. I start by
empathically connecting to what
needs of theirs are being met by doing
what they do. Then I let them know
what need of mine is not being met by
what they're doing—the fear that I feel
by how they behave, or the discomfort
I feel. And then we explore other ways
that are more effective and less costly
of meeting both of our needs.

*The practice
of NVC is very
much in harmony
with principles
of restorative
justice.*

This is an example of why those of
us who practice NVC also are very much in harmony with
principles of restorative justice. The idea is that if we really
want to have peace and harmony, we have to find out what
will restore peace and not just punish the bad guys. Much of
our training is in harmony with these principles. Sometimes
restorative justice takes the form of my meeting with a person
who has had some terrible experiences with another person.

For example, the person might have been raped. Instead
of simply punishing this person for doing it, it is established
by agreement on both sides that restorative justice will be
attempted. Often this person is in prison and has a choice
whether to engage in restorative justice.

How does it work? I start by helping the person who has

been victimized express the pain they've experienced. And it's often deep. Very deep. And they don't know our training, so they don't know how to express it in a gentle way. This might be a woman who's been raped who screams pretty strong things at this person: "I'd like you to die. I want you to be tortured. You know, you're a pig."

Then I help the person who did this connect empathically with the suffering of the other person, really just to hear the depth of what that person has suffered. They're not used to that. The first thing they want to do is apologize.

Connect empathically with the suffering of the other person.

They say, "I'm sorry. You know ..."

I interrupt and say, "No, hold it. Remember what I said before. I want empathy first. I want you to show her that you fully understand the depth of her suffering. Can you repeat back her feelings and needs?"

They can't. I say, "Let me repeat it." And I transform all of what she said into her feelings and needs. Then I help the other person to hear it. The person who has been raped is experiencing understanding from the person who did it. Then I help him mourn for what he did. Not apologize; that's too easy. I help him go inside and look at what he feels when he sees the suffering of this other person. That requires going deeply into oneself. It's very painful, but it's a healing kind of pain. So I help him do that.

Of course, the other person is witnessing this person now

sincerely mourning, not just apologizing. And then I ask, "What was going on in you when you did this to her?" I help him articulate it in terms of feelings and needs, and I help the victim empathize with that. At that point there are two different people in the room than the two who came in.

EXERCISE:

In relation to the person who has done something you don't like, think of the ways they might have met their needs without doing what hurt you. Write down how you might express those options to them, using what we have covered so far.

CHAPTER · 8

GANGS AND OTHER DOMINATION STRUCTURES

HOW WE GOT WHERE WE ARE

*"The world will change for the better when
people decide they are sick and tired of being
sick and tired of the way the world is,
and decide to change themselves."*

— SIDNEY MADWED

W E'VE SEEN HOW NONVIOLENT COMMUNICATION helps us bring about change within ourselves, as well as change with other people. And we know it requires a *need consciousness.* It requires awareness that *all* blame and *all* judgments—like *I'm dirty,* like *I'm an alcoholic,* like *I'm an addict*—get in the way of learning and make it hard to learn more effective ways of living at less cost. Now let's take a look at how this awareness might apply to more than individuals.

First, a bit of history. According to people like historical theologian Walter Wink, about eight to ten thousand years ago for various reasons a myth developed that the good life was good people punishing and conquering bad people. And this myth seemed to support living under authoritarian regimes, the leaders of which might call themselves kings or czars. And these *domination societies,* as I call them (where the people who think they are superior control others), excel at programming people to think in ways that make nice, dead people out of them. They'll do what people tell them.

> *Domination societies excel at programming people to think in ways that make nice, dead people out of them.*

Women will believe that nice women have no needs; they sacrifice their needs for their family. Brave men have no needs; they're willing to lose their lives to protect the king's property. At the same time we developed this way of thinking, of judging one another in ways that imply that reward is justified and punishment is justified. We created judicial systems based on *retributive* justice that reinforce the idea that reward and punishment are deserved. I believe that this way of thinking and behaving is at the core of violence on our planet.

If you want to maintain authoritarian structures, it helps to educate people to believe that some things are right, and some things are wrong, good, bad, selfish, unselfish. And who knows what these are? The person at the top of the hierarchy, of course. So, your mind gets programmed to worry about how you're being judged by the person who's higher on the authority pyramid than you are.

This mindset is not very difficult to cultivate, because all it requires is getting people disconnected from what's really alive in them and other people—to get them worrying about how they're going to be judged by other people. So, living under these authorities, we develop language that disconnects us from ourselves and other people, all of which makes compassion very difficult.

We still have a domination society, except that we have substituted an oligarchy for a king. We have what I call a *gang* dominating us rather than an individual. In many of our social-change efforts, we are seemingly concerned with the actions of groups of people rather than individual behaviors. In my way of thinking, gangs are groups that behave in ways we don't like. Some gangs call themselves street gangs. They're not the ones that scare me the most.

> *Gangs are groups that behave in ways we don't like.*
>
> ∞

Other gangs call themselves multinational corporations. Some gangs call themselves governments. These last two often do things as gangs that conflict with the values I embrace. These gangs control the schools, and many of them want the teachers to teach students that there's a right and a wrong, a good and a bad. They want schools to make students work for rewards so they can be hired later on to work eight hours a day for forty years of their life doing meaningless tasks.

Basically, it's the same structure as before; it's just that we've substituted a gang for a king. For further reading on this subject, I recommend G. William Domhoff's book *Who Rules America?* He's a political science professor who lost two jobs writing the book because the people in the gang have a lot of money, and they don't like to fund professors to educate the public about their gang.

Having said that, I don't think the people caught up in domination systems from the very beginning are bad people overtly trying to manipulate the masses. Rather, they have developed the structure, they believe it, they believe that they are blessed with being somehow closer to higher authority, and they're doing this to preserve this higher authority's presence on the earth.

> *NVC offers a game that's much more fun to play than dominating other people.*
>
>

It's just a long-standing way of looking at the world that most of the world has been exposed to, but not all of the world. Ruth Benedict, Margaret Mead, and other anthropologists show that there are whole parts of the world that haven't been exposed to this way of thinking. These areas experience far less violence.

Nonviolent Communication offers people caught up in domination systems a way of thinking and communicating that I'm sure would make their life much more wonderful. We can show them a game that's much more fun to play than dominating other people and creating wars. Really, there's a much more enjoyable way to live!

So let's look at how Nonviolent Communication can help us transform "gangs." I encourage an awareness of how gang behavior affects how we are educated, what we carry within our self. Let me show you what I mean. I've been suggesting that certain language and certain forms of communication have been very destructive. But where did this language come from? Where did the predominance of moralistic judgments and the tactics of punishment and reward come from? Why do we use them? We learn these tactics because they support certain gang behaviors.

CREATING CHANGE IN OUR SCHOOLS

"If we don't change direction soon,
we'll end up where we're going."

— IRWIN COREY

For example, let's look at our schools. According to Michael B. Katz, educational historian studying educational change, we're on about a twenty-year cycle of reform. About every twenty years citizens start to get concerned and, at great risk, make educational changes that are good from the standpoint of raising learning levels and reducing problems like violence in the schools.

They initiate changes, but within five years the changes

they instituted are gone. In his book *Class, Bureaucracy, and Schools*, Katz shows why he thinks this is so. He says the problem is that the reformers try to show what's wrong with schools and try to change that. They don't see what's right with them.

U.S. schools, however, are doing what they were set up to do, which is to support gang behavior. Which gang? In this case, it's the economic-structure gang, the people who control our businesses. They control our schools, and they have three historical goals:

First, to teach people obedience to authority so that when they get hired they'll do what they're told.

Second, they get people to work for extrinsic rewards. They want people to learn not how to enrich their lives, but to receive grades, to be rewarded with a better high-paying job in the future. If you're a gang who wants to hire a person to put out a product or service that doesn't really serve life (but makes a lot of money for the owners of this gang), you want workers who aren't asking themselves, *Is this product we're turning out really serving life?* No, you just want them to do what they're told and to work for a salary.

Katz says the third function of our schools—and this really makes lasting change difficult—is that they're doing a good job of maintaining a caste system and making it look like a democracy.

It's the structure that's the problem, not individuals. Teachers and administrators within the schools are not enemies. They genuinely want to contribute to children's well-being. There are no enemies here. It's the gang structure we have set up to maintain our economy. So what do we do if we want to transform the schools in ways that better serve people? We need not only to change the schools, we also need to change the bigger structure of which schools are a part.

> *The structure is the problem, not individuals. Teachers and administrators are not the enemies.*
>
> ∞

The good news is that it can happen. We're now working in several countries to make radical transformations in schools. We're supporting schools, teachers, and students to work in harmony with the principles of Nonviolent Communication. I'm pleased to say that we have many teachers supporting the creation of such schools now in Serbia, Italy, Israel, Costa Rica, and elsewhere around the world. Of course, the vision is that the radical transformation will carry through to the consciousness of the next generation of children.

Let me give you an example of how we can teach NVC to young children just like anybody else. The theory is that, if they're having conflicts, then they can use NVC to mediate their conflicts. I was recently in an Israeli kindergarten where children normally begin between 4 and 6 years old. Two young girls were squabbling. I didn't understand their language, but they were arguing, all right, and they said something to a young boy. I asked my interpreter to come over, and she said the girls were asking the boy to mediate. I said, "What?"

The three of them—all kindergartners—ran off to the mediation corner of the room, and the mediator asked the one girl what she was observing, what the other child had said that she didn't like. "How do you feel?" he asked, and she said how she felt.

"What are your needs?" he continued, then later, "What is your request?"

> "If I didn't see it, I wouldn't believe it."
>
> ∞

He really helped her. He asked her the basic questions of Nonviolent Communication. They had all studied it, so the girl didn't have any trouble answering the questions. Then he asked the other girl to repeat back what the first one had said. Then when the first child was understood, the mediator helped the other girl express herself and helped this girl hear the other side. In a short time they had resolved the conflict and run off together. A woman from the Netherlands (who was there with me and sharing the same interpreter) said to me, "If I didn't see it, I wouldn't believe it."

We teach students to mediate as well. They can do it. Indeed, they can do it very well—at all ages.

Working with Gangs in Ghettos

"At the present time, the alternative is not between
change or no change, but between change for
the better and change for the worse."

— Clifford Hugh Douglas

I was in the inner city of St. Louis where I worked and lived at the time, talking to the minister in a black church in the heart of the ghetto. The warlord of a street gang heard there was this white man talking to people on his turf, and he wanted to be in on it. So, he just walked into this meeting in the minister's office. He sat there staring at me talking to the people about this process of communication that I was offering them to help with race relations. After a while he said, "We don't need no great white father coming down to teach us how to communicate. We know how to communicate. You want to help us, give us your money so we can buy guns and get rid of fools like you!"

I had heard things like that before, and I wasn't in a particularly good mood that day, so instead of practicing what I teach, I got into a competitive harangue with him. It wasn't going well, and I soon saw what I was doing, so I stopped, came back to life, and began applying our training. I tried to hear just what he, the human being, was feeling and needing.

> *I stopped,*
> *came back to*
> *life, and began*
> *applying our*
> *training.*

I shifted and said, "So you'd like some respect for how the people here communicate, and you'd also like some awareness of how other people have oppressed those people they originally say they're going to help." Instead of competing with him, I just tried to understand his feelings and needs. This shifted things. He just sat there and stared the rest of the meeting.

When the meeting was over, it was dark outside, and I started walking to my car. It's always a little risky being a white person in that neighborhood. Then I heard, "Rosenberg!" and thought to myself, *Uh-oh, I got smart too late.* "Give me a ride," he said, then told me where he wanted to go.

He got into the car and went right to that moment where I shifted to try to understand him rather than compete with him. He said, "What were you doing to me in there?"

I said, "That's the process I was talking about."

Then he said something that changed both our lives for the next thirteen years. He said, "Can you teach me how to teach that to the Zulus?" (That was the name of his gang.) "We're not going to beat you white people with guns. We're going to have to learn stuff like that."

I said, "I'll trade you. I'll teach you how to teach this to the Zulus if you go to Washington with me on Thursday where I've been invited to work with the school system to show them why the blacks are burning down the schools."

He laughed and said, "Hey, man, I got no education."

I said, "Look, if you can pick this up the way you did just now, you've got a fine education. You may not have had much schooling, but you had a good education."

He went with me to Washington and did an incredible job of helping administrators and teachers understand why kids were burning down the schools. For the next thirteen years we did a lot of work together all over the South, preparing schools for desegregation. The federal government asked us to go into some pretty hot areas and do conflict resolution between blacks and whites. He became the head of public housing in the city of St. Louis. Another member of the same gang almost became mayor of St. Louis several years back.

Changing Other Social Institutions

"Vision without action is merely a dream.
Action without vision just passes the time.
Vision with action can change the world."

Joel Barker

What about other big gangs? Along with the schools, another major area of change for us is with the judicial system, with the government gangs that operate the legal system. We know from research in the United States that if two people are convicted of the same offense, and one goes into our prisons and one doesn't, the one who goes into prison is more likely to behave in a violent way upon getting out than the one who doesn't go to prison.

We know that the people who receive capital punishment are far more likely to be low-income, or people of color. We know that this is horrible, but it happens—and that it's the system, the gang, that needs to change. The individuals within it are not monsters, but as members of a gang they need to change. I hope that by now everybody is aware of the failure of the punitive structures that are part of our judicial system. There needs to be a transition from *retributive* justice to *restorative* justice.

There needs to be a transition from retributive justice to restorative justice.

Where do we find the energy and skill to work for social change? When we have been so affected internally by these gangs, it's all we can do just to get ourselves and our own families in order. After we work on our self to transform the world within and try to make human connections with people around us, how do we have enough energy left to tackle these larger gangs?

EXERCISE:

Think of one thing you can do to make it more likely that you'll attempt to change something you don't like. Write this down and put it in a place to remind yourself to do it.

CHAPTER · 9

TRANSFORMING ENEMY IMAGES AND CONNECTING

*"The greatest revolution in our generation
is that of human beings, who by changing the
inner attitudes of their minds, can change
the outer aspects of their lives."*

— MARILYN FERGUSON

IN OUR TRAINING WE WANT PEOPLE NOT ONLY TO COME OUT with awareness of how Nonviolent Communication can be used to transform our inner world, we want people to see how it can be used to create the world outside that we want to live in. We can show we do have the power, we do have the energy, or at least we can get it. How do we do that?

First, we need to liberate ourselves from *enemy* images, the thinking that says there is something wrong with the people who are part of these gangs. Now, that's not easy to do. It's hard to see that those who are doing these things are human beings like the rest of us. It's very challenging with

> *We need to liberate ourselves from enemy images.*
>
>

gangs, and often it's just as difficult with individuals.

Let me give you an example. I was in Fargo, North Dakota, to work in the schools, not to do mediation. Somebody who had helped us get into the schools asked me a personal favor. She said, "You know, Marshall, in my family we're having a big conflict about my father's retirement. He wants to retire, but there's tremendous conflict in the family between my two brothers about how my father wants to divide up our large farm. We've even been in the courts trying to solve this. It's horrible. I could arrange your schedule so you could have a long lunch of two and a half hours. Would you be willing to mediate?"

I said, "You say it's been going on for months?"

She said, "Actually years, and I know it's over lunchtime, Marshall, but whatever you could do to help, I would really appreciate it."

So I went into the room that day with the father and the brothers. Incidentally, the father lived in the middle of the farm, and each son lived on one end. The brothers hadn't spoken to each other in eight years! I asked the usual question to the brothers: "Could you tell me what your needs are?"

The younger brother suddenly screamed at his older brother, "You know, you've never been fair to me. You and Dad only care about each other. You've never cared about me."

Then the older brother said, "Well, you never did the work."

And so they were yelling at each other for about two minutes. I didn't need to hear more about the background. In that short amount of time, I could guess what each side's needs were that weren't being addressed or understood.

> *In that short amount of time, I could guess what each side's needs were.*

Because I was pressed for time, I said to the older brother, "Excuse me. Could I play your role for a moment?"

He looked a little puzzled, but he shrugged and said, "Go ahead."

So I played his role as though he had Nonviolent Communication skills. I was able to hear behind the younger brother's judgmental way of expressing himself what his needs were that weren't met. And I'd heard enough of the older brother's needs by then to express his needs in a different way. And we made a lot of progress in helping the brothers see each other's needs. However, the two and a half hours were up, and I had to go back and do my workshop.

The next morning, the father—who, as I noted, had been sitting in on the session—came to where I was working with the teachers. He was waiting for me out in the hall. He had tears in his eyes, and he said, "Thank you so much for what you did yesterday. We all went out to dinner last night for the first time in eight years, and we resolved the conflict over dinner."

Getting past the enemy images is the hard work.

See? Once both sides get over the enemy image and recognize each other's needs, it's amazing how the next part, which is looking for strategies to meet everyone's needs, becomes pretty easy by comparison. It's getting past the enemy images that's the hard work. It's getting people to see that you can't benefit at other people's expense. Once you have *that* clear, even complicated things like family squabbles aren't horrible to resolve because you've got people connecting at a human level.

The same thing applies to gangs. The most common elements I've found in the conflicts I've been asked to mediate are that people—instead of knowing how to say clearly what their needs and requests are—are quite eloquent in diagnosing other people's pathology: what's wrong with them for behaving as they do. Whether it's two individuals, two groups, or two countries that have conflicts, they begin the discussion with enemy images, telling the other person what's wrong with them. The divorce courts—and the bombs—are never far away.

Mediating between Warring Tribes

"It is not necessary to change.
Survival is not mandatory."

— W. Edwards Deming

I once was asked to help mediate a conflict between two tribes in northern Nigeria—between Christian chiefs and Muslim chiefs. These tribes had a lot of violence going on between them because of a conflict over how many locations in the marketplace each tribe would have to display its wares. One hundred of the four hundred people in this community had been killed the year I arrived.

A colleague of mine who lives in Nigeria, seeing all this violence, worked very hard to meet the chiefs on both sides and get them to agree to meet and see if we could resolve this conflict. It took him six months, but he finally was successful, and that's how I came to be working with the chiefs of these tribes.

As we were walking into the session, my colleague whispered to me, "Be prepared for some tension, Marshall. Three of the people who are going to be in the meeting know that someone who killed their child is in the room."

Well, it *was* very tense at first. There had been so much violence between these two groups, and this was the first time they had sat down together. Now there were twelve chiefs on one side of the table, twelve on the other. I started as I usually do in mediation. I said, "I'm confident that if anybody's

Unfortunately, people don't know how to express needs.

needs get expressed and understood, we'll find a way to get everybody's needs met. So who would like to begin, please? I'd like to hear what needs of yours are not being met."

Unfortunately, they didn't know how to express needs. They only knew how to express criticism and judgments. Instead of responding to my question, a chief from the Christian tribe yelled loudly and angrily across the table at the Muslims, "You people are murderers!"

(Notice I did not say, "What do you think of the other side?")

So I asked, "What needs of yours are not getting met?" Right away, there was the enemy image.

Then, immediately, the other side came back: "You've been trying to dominate us." There's another diagnosis. With those kinds of enemy images, I could see why thirty percent of the population had been killed over the question of how many places in the marketplace each side will get.

They're screaming at each other, and it wasn't easy to restore order. But our training shows that all criticisms, judgments, and enemy images are tragic, even suicidal, expressions of unmet needs. So in the world of mediation I loan them my Nonviolent Communication skills by translating their enemy image into a need. With the gentleman who said, "You're murderers," it wasn't too hard.

I asked, "Chief, are you expressing a need for safety that

isn't being met? You have a need for safety. You would hope that no matter what's going on, things could be resolved with nonviolence, correct?"

> *It's closer to the truth to hear needs than the enemy image.*

He said, "That's exactly what I'm saying."

Well, that wasn't quite what he was saying. He said, "You're murderers." But it's closer to the truth to hear the needs than the enemy image. With Nonviolent Communication skills, I was able to hear the needs behind the judgment.

But that wasn't enough. I had to be sure his needs were heard by the other side. So I asked if a member of the other tribe would be willing to repeat what the chief from the first tribe had said. I looked over across the table to the Muslim chiefs and said, "Would somebody from this side of the table please tell me back what the chief said his needs were?"

And one of them screams over, "Why did you kill my son?"

And I said to the chief from the second side, "Chief, we'll deal with that issue soon. For the moment, would you be willing to tell me what the first chief's feelings and needs are?"

Well, of course, he couldn't do it. He was so involved in making judgments of the other side that he wasn't able to hear the feelings and needs that I had helped articulate.

So I said to this chief, "Chief, what I hear the other chief feeling is anger, strong anger, because he says he has a need for conflicts, whatever they are, to be resolved in some way—other than with violence—so everybody can be safe.

Could you just say that back, Chief, so I'm sure we're communicating?"

He wasn't able to do it yet. I had to repeat the message at least two more times before he heard what the other chief was feeling and needing. Finally, he was able to tell me.

Then I helped the other chiefs express their needs. I asked, "Now that you hear what the needs are of the other side, I'd like you to tell me your needs."

And one of the chiefs repeated the judgment he had made earlier by saying, "They have been trying to dominate us for a long time, and we're not going to put up with it anymore."

Once again I translated this judgment of the wrongness of the other side into the needs I sensed to be at the root of this judgment by asking, "Are you upset because you have a strong need for equality in this community?"

He said, "Yes."

I turned to a member of the other tribe and said, "Could you repeat that so I'm sure that we're communicating?"

> *If we can just say our needs without putting it in an enemy image, we can resolve conflicts peacefully.*
>
>

They were not able to at first. I had to repeat that at least another two times before they were able to see that the other side had anger related to a need for equality that wasn't being met.

All took about an hour just to get each side clear about their needs and to get the other side to hear them, because there was a lot of yelling and screaming going on in between. However, at that point, when I got both sides just to hear one need from each other, one of the chiefs jumped up to his feet and said to me, "Marshall, we can't learn this in one day. And if we know how to talk to each other this way, we don't have to kill each other."

You see? He understood in one hour or so that if we can just say what our needs are without putting it in an enemy image, we can resolve conflicts peacefully.

And I said, "Chief, I'm glad you could see that so quickly. We were going to suggest at the end of the day that we would be glad to train people from both tribes to use this in case other conflicts come up. However, today I'm here to mediate the conflicts; I wasn't here to teach you. And yes, you're right. It can't be learned in one day."

He said, "I want to be one of those trained to do this."

Several others in the room also were eager to volunteer to get the training. They could see that you don't need weapons to resolve conflicts when you know how to connect clearly with each other's needs.

ADDRESSING TERRORISM

*"Those who make peaceful revolution impossible
will make violent revolution inevitable."*

— JOHN F. KENNEDY

Many people have asked me how we can use NVC to address terrorism. For starters, we need to get rid of images of *terrorist* and *freedom fighter*. As long as we are thinking of the other side as terrorists and ourselves as freedom fighters, we're part of the problem. Then we need to empathize with what was alive in these people when they did what they did that's so frightening and hurtful to us—and to see what human needs they were trying to meet by doing it.

Until we can empathically connect with that, whatever actions we take are likely to come out of an energy that's going to create more violence.

Now, with regard to the people who have done things we call "terrorism," I'm confident they have been expressing their pain in many different ways for thirty years or more. Instead of our empathically receiving it when they expressed it in much gentler ways—they were trying to tell us how hurt they felt that some of their most sacred needs were not being respected by the way we were trying to meet our economic and military needs—they

*Instead of
thinking of them
as terrorists,
we need to
empathize.*

got progressively more agitated. Finally, they got so agitated that it took horrible form.

So that's the first thing. Instead of thinking of them as terrorists, we need to empathize. Many people hear that as saying terrorism is OK—that we should just smile and act like it's OK to kill thousands of people.

Not at all! After we empathize, we need to make clear what our pain is, what needs of ours weren't met by their actions. And if we can have that connection with these people, we can find a way to get everybody's needs met peacefully. But if we label them as terrorists and then try to punish them for being terrorists, we already see what we're going to get. Violence creates more violence.

That's why the first thing we do with people when we're training them in how to tackle "terrorist gangs" is how to do the necessary *despair work*: looking inside and dealing with your own pain in relationship to the gangs. You transform *all* the enemy images you have of other people into clarity about what needs of yours are not getting met.

Then we show people that no matter what the level of social change—even if you're trying to tackle a big gang like a government or multinational corporation—basically it boils down to momentum and numbers. The change will occur when a significant number of people within that gang radically change how they see things, when they see more effective ways of getting their human needs met than continuing the gang behavior. Again, we try to get change, not by destroying existing structures, but by connecting with

> *Change will occur when people radically change how they see things, when they see more effective ways of getting their needs met.*

people within those structures to find more effective, less costly ways of meeting their needs (that meet the needs of others as well).

We want to change some multinational corporations and their practices. We don't want to convince them that they're evil people because they are destroying the environment and oppressing people from other countries by their hiring and trade practices. We want to connect with the people within these "corporate gangs" to show them how you cannot meet your own needs at other people's expense. We want to help them get clear what their needs are and to find other ways of transforming their organization to better meet their needs at less cost to themselves and other people. The same thing applies to individuals, families, and groups of every size and complexity.

Now, this kind of communication can be time-consuming and difficult. It could be that it's not only one or two people with whom we need to have this connection and this transformative experience. Changing some gang behavior might require millions of people to act differently. For example, if this gang is a government, we might need to get a certain percentage of the population to see more effective ways of meeting their needs than the present gang is using.

Sometimes the gang might be four or five people who

control it from the top positions, and if they can see other ways of getting their needs met that are less costly and more effective, then the social change we want we can come about fairly quickly. In any event, once you're talking about gangs, transformation is usually far more than one person can do.

Peace requires something far more difficult than revenge or merely turning the other cheek; it requires empathizing with the fears and unmet needs that provide the impetus for people to attack each other. Being aware of these feelings and needs, people lose their desire to attack back because they can see the human ignorance leading to these attacks; instead, their goal becomes providing the empathic connection and education that will enable them to transcend their violence and engage in cooperative relationships.

> *Peace requires something far more difficult than revenge or merely turning the other cheek.*

When people get connected to their needs, they don't have this anger that drives them to want to punish others. We do need to make evaluations about our needs: Are they being met or not? But we do this without going up into our heads and making enemies and villains out of the people who in some way are not fulfilling our needs.

Every time we go up into our head and make a judgment of others instead of going into our heart and seeing the needs, we decrease the likelihood that other people will enjoy giving to us.

The fact remains that when people get connected to the needs behind the anger, frustration, and violence, they move into a different world. They're in the world that Rumi, the thirteenth-century Sufi mystic and poet, talks about: "Out beyond ideas of rightdoing and wrongdoing there is a field: I'll meet you there."

PART III

SPEAKING PEACE
FOR SOCIAL CHANGE

"Peace is a daily, a weekly, a monthly process,
gradually changing opinions, slowly eroding
old barriers, quietly building new structures.
And however undramatic the pursuit
of peace, the pursuit must go on."

— JOHN F. KENNEDY

CHAPTER · 10

JOINING FORCES WITH OTHERS TO CREATE SOCIAL CHANGE

"Never doubt that a small group of
committed people can change the world.
It is the only thing that ever has."

— MARGARET MEAD

A BIG PART OF HELPING SOCIAL CHANGE HAPPEN IS connecting with other people who share a similar vision. We show how Nonviolent Communication can be used to identify the structures you want to produce in cooperation with people who share the vision of the world you would like to create. We show how to build a team that works together to bring about these changes.

One thing that often happens in the beginning with these teams is that they have battles among themselves. We often carry within ourselves skills that don't lend themselves to good teamwork. So here we are trying to change outside

We show social-change teams how to use NVC to work better as a team to make meetings more productive.

structures that seem very large. This naturally seems to be a big task, and it becomes even more difficult when our group struggles from within. So in training for social-change efforts we show social-change teams how to use Nonviolent Communication to work better as a team in order to make their meetings more productive.

For example, I was working with a team of minority citizens in San Francisco that was most concerned about the schools their children were attending. Their interpretation of the schools was that they were destroying the spirit of their children. There were certain structures they wanted to change.

However, they said to me, "Marshall, the problem is that we've been getting together for about six months to try to create social change, but all we do is get into arguments or unproductive discussions, and we never get anywhere. Can you show us how Nonviolent Communication can help us build a team, help us make more effective use of our meetings?"

So I went to their meeting and said, "Have your usual meeting, and I'll observe, then I'll see if I can help show you how Nonviolent Communication can be used in making your teamwork more effective."

The meeting began with a man who had clipped an article out of the newspaper. It was an article of how parents were accusing a principal of abusing one of their children. The principal was a white person, and the child was a minority person. He read this article, then another man responded to it and said, "That's nothing. I went to that same school when I was a kid, and let me tell you what happened to me."

And then for the next ten minutes everybody was talking about things that had happened to them in the past, what a racist system it was, and so forth.

I let this go on for a bit, and then I said, "Could I break in here? I'd like to ask you all to raise your hand if you have found the meeting productive to this point." Not one hand went up— not even by those individuals who had told stories.

> *You can't afford to burn up your energy with unproductive meetings.*

This group of people had been getting together to bring about change in a system, but they had been having discussions that nobody found productive. These people had to leave their families to come to that meeting. It wasn't easy to find the time and energy. When we're trying to tackle gang structure for social change, we can't afford to burn up our energy with unproductive meetings.

So I went back to the gentleman who had started the conversation, and I said, "Sir, can you tell me your request of the group? What did you want back from the group when you read that article from the newspaper?"

> *Be sure you end whatever you're saying with clarity about what you want back.*
>
>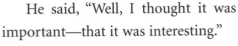

He said, "Well, I thought it was important—that it was interesting."

I said, "I'm sure you thought it was interesting, but you're telling me what you think. I'm asking what you wanted back from the group ..."

He said, "I don't know what I wanted."

And I said, "That's why I think we had ten minutes of unproductive discussion. Whenever we take the attention of a group and present something, and we're not clear what we want, it's very likely that we're not going to have a very productive encounter. Nonviolent Communication shows us, whether we're talking with an individual or a group, to be sure you end whatever you're saying with clarity about what you want back: What is your request?

Presenting your pain or thoughts without a clear request is very likely to be the stimulus for an unproductive discussion." This is one of several ways we show people how Nonviolent Communication can be useful in making their meetings more productive.

I was working with another team of minority citizens who wanted to change hiring practices in a different gang in San Francisco: the health services department of city government. These citizens felt that the hiring practices were oppressive because they discriminated against certain people. They wanted me to show them how Nonviolent

Communication could be helpful to them in getting their needs better met by that gang.

For three days I showed them the process and how it could be used—and then they were to go out that afternoon and come back the next morning, and we would see how it went. The next morning they came back very discouraged, and one of them said, "We knew it wouldn't work. There's no way to change this system."

I said, "OK. I can see you're really discouraged."

"Yes, yes."

"So, tell me what happened so we can learn from this."

The team of six of them had gone into an administrator's office, and they told me how they had used Nonviolent Communication very well. They hadn't gone in and diagnosed the system as oppressive. Rather, first they had made a real clear observation of what was going on. They identified the law that they felt was discriminatory because it didn't allow for the hiring of certain people.

Second, they expressed their feelings, how painful it was for them because they needed work and equality. They believed they could do this work, and it was painful for them to be excluded. They made a clear request of the administrator, saying exactly how they would like to see the hiring practices changed to better allow for them to be hired.

They told me how they said it, and I was very pleased. They incorporated beautifully the training we had gone through. They had stated clearly what their needs were, what their requests were, and they didn't use insulting language. I said, "I like how you expressed that, but what was his response?"

And they said, "Oh, he was very nice, you know. He even thanked us for coming in. He said it's very important in a democracy that the citizens express themselves, and we encourage that in this organization, but at the moment your request is quite unrealistic, and I'm sorry that it won't be possible right now, but thank you for coming in."

And I said, "Then what did you do?"

"Well, we left."

> *Hear behind that bureaucratic-ese to what is in their heart.*
>
>

I said, "Wait a minute. Wait a minute. What about the other half that I showed you? How to hear behind that bureaucratic-ese to what was in his heart, what he was feeling, what his needs were? Where was that human being in relationship to what you wanted?"

One of them said, "We know what was going on in him. He wanted us to get out of there."

"Well, even if that's true, what was going on in him? What was he feeling? What were his needs? He's a human being. What was that human being feeling and needing?"

They forgot to see his humanness because he is within a structure. And within the structure he was speaking structure language, not human language. He spoke the language of bureaucracy. As Walter Wink points out, organizations, structures, and governments have their own spirituality. And within those environments people communicate in a way that supports that spirituality.

Nonviolent Communication shows us a way, no matter what the structure, to cut through it and see the human being within it. I could see that I hadn't trained them well enough on how to do that, so we practiced. We practiced how to hear the needs behind all that burcaucratic language, how to see the human being and make a connection that strengthens our ability to work toward social change with that person.

After our training at that level, they made another appointment with this man. And they came back the next morning delighted. When they saw what was behind his messages, they saw that he was scared. He actually shared their needs—he didn't like to see how this law was discriminatory—but he had another need: to protect himself.

> *Work together in ways that get everybody's needs met.*

And he knew that his boss would be very upset with this suggestion, because his boss was vehemently opposed to what they were after. He had a need to protect himself, and didn't want to go to the boss and help them make the change. Once this team of citizens saw what his needs were, they worked together, but in a way that got everybody's needs met.

What happened is that he mentored them. He led them through what they would need to go through to get what they wanted, and they met his need by protecting him, by not letting anybody know that he was mentoring them. Eventually, they all got the change in the structure that they wanted.

Effective social change requires connections with others in which we avoid seeing the people within these structures as enemies—and we to try to hear the needs of the human beings within. Then we persist in keeping the flow of communication going so that everybody's needs get met.

EXERCISE:

Think of someone you'd like to connect with, but whom you now consider to be an enemy. What's the first thing you'll do to turn that conflict into connection?

Funding for Social Change

"I cannot say whether things will get better
if we change; what I can say is they must
change if they are to get better."

— Georg Lichtenberg

Another social-change project I worked on involved the street gang I talked about earlier. The leader of this gang (Zulus) thought what I was offering, if adjusted to his culture, could be very helpful. As I mentioned earlier, we did a lot of work together over the years on school desegregation throughout the United States.

One thing we wanted to do together was create a school that would show how teachers and students could work as partners to educate the students who were being kicked out or pushed out of schools, rather than the teachers trying to control the students.

We wanted to start with a demonstration school in which we would show we could reach these rejected students who usually weren't making it in other schools. Then we'd use this as a stepping-stone toward broader changes in the school system. This first part required us to raise fifty thousand dollars to pay the teachers and cover other program costs.

This is a very important part of social change: How do you get the resources you need? I learned a valuable lesson from this gang member in how to make the best use of a short period of time when you are engaged in social-change efforts.

This is very important because there's obviously a lot of communication that needs to go on in social-change efforts. So we need not only to speak Nonviolent Communication from the heart, we need to be brief and clear and make the most of short periods of time—or, as they're sometimes called, windows of opportunity.

You need to be brief and clear and make the most of short periods of time.

This is the good lesson I learned from my gang-member friend. He said to me, "Why don't we go to that foundation that you've been doing some work for; they give money. Why can't we go down there and get the money for this project?"

"Yeah," I said, "I sure would like them to do it, but I know right now that they don't accept applications for another couple of months. This quarter is over. Not only that, in order to get money from them you have to have a big proposal and, you know, we don't have the time or the resources right now to get that kind of proposal ready."

He said, "Yeah, yeah. That's one way to do it, but can you get the appointment?"

I said, "Yeah, I can probably get the appointment with this person."

He said, "Well, get the appointment, and let's go down there and get the money."

I said, "What are you going to do if I get the appointment?"

He said, "Let me handle it. Let me handle it."

So I called up, and I said, "This is Dr. Rosenberg. I was

working last month with the administrators and … could I have a meeting with the president?"

And the secretary said, "Well, you know he's very busy, Dr. Rosenberg, but I'll see and call you back."

So she called me back and said, "We can fit you in between meetings. He'll be glad to see you, but it'll only be about twenty minutes. How's that, Dr. Rosenberg?"

I said, "Thank you, that will work."

So, as we were driving to the meeting, I said to my colleague, "Now, what are you going to do during this twenty minutes?"

He said, "Let me handle it. Let me handle it." So, we get into the meeting and I politely introduced the two of them. I said, "Dr. X, this is my colleague Al, and Al, this is Dr. X."

Al reached over, shook his hand, and said, "Hi, brother. Where's the money?"

Now, I could've beaten him on the head with a broom, I was so embarrassed that he would start a professional meeting like this. My usual approach to soliciting funds would've been to go in with a proposal and slides and to try to document all the value of what we were trying to do to get the money.

But this man was starting just the opposite. He was saying, in effect, *We're here to get some money; what do you need to hear from us to decide whether you want to give it or not?* The president, in a very polite way, laughed and said, "What money?" And my colleague said, "Money for the fun school."

"The fun school … what's that?"

"It's a school Rosenberg and our gang is setting up to show that kids kicked out of school can make it if they're treated differently."

What do you need to hear from us to give us what we came for?

"What will this fun school be like?" Notice what my friend had done. In our precious time, instead of going in and filling the air with what we think the other person needs to hear, in his cultural style Al started off from the very beginning by essentially saying to the other person *what do you need to hear from us to give us what we came for?* He let the other person direct where the conversation went. We walked out with fifty thousand dollars.

Over the years since that happened, which was about thirty years ago, I have used that approach repeatedly in my social-change efforts. Not necessarily starting as Al did in his cultural style, but setting it up in the very beginning that the other person can find out from me what they need to hear to decide whether or not they want to support the change that I'm interested in.

I used that approach once with a key committee in Sweden made up of top government and business leaders. My colleague and I wanted to talk to them about supporting a social-change project. It took some effort to get an appointment with this committee, but they finally agreed to give us twenty minutes. While my colleague and I were waiting, a secretary came out and said, "Dr. Rosenberg, I apologize, but the committee wants me to tell you that they're running a little late. Instead of the twenty minutes they said they could allot you, they have only five."

OK, well, if I have only five minutes, all the more reason to use what I learned from my colleague Al. So I went into the meeting and told them exactly what I hoped they would agree to—and asked what they needed to know from me to decide in five minutes whether they wanted to agree to it. Then they took forty minutes asking questions! But even if they had only given me five minutes, I think I got more out of it by letting them tell me what they needed to hear rather than my using a lot of words that weren't going to help.

Here's another application of Nonviolent Communication for social change. In our meetings we can be more productive and not fill the air with a lot of words. Rather, we can create a flow in which the other person can tell us what they need to know to decide whether we can work together.

Don't fill the air with a lot of words. Rather, create a flow in which the other person can tell you what they need to know.

EXERCISE:

The next time you're involved in an unproductive meeting, what can you do to get things moving? (Hint: Focus on observations, feelings, needs, and clear requests!)

CHAPTER · 11

DEALING WITH CONFLICT
AND CONFRONTATION

*"It is the acid test of nonviolence that in a
nonviolent conflict there is no rancor left behind,
and in the end the enemies are
converted into friends."*

— M.K. GANDHI

S OCIAL CHANGE, OF COURSE, IS GOING TO INVOLVE
considerable confrontation at times. We need to learn
how to use Nonviolent Communication when we're up
against people who are opposed to what we're after, but who
don't know how to express themselves in a way that clearly
communicates their feelings and needs. We need to know
(under these confrontational conditions) how to hear people's
feelings and needs, no matter how they're communicating.

One example of this was in a social-change project in
Illinois. It involved a public school we had created, but we
wanted to go from this school to the whole system

> *We need to know how to hear people's feelings and needs, no matter how they're communicating.*

functioning in harmony, using the principles of the school. It was very hard to get this school going, but after much resistance, we finally did get federal funding that allowed us to start the school.

However, in the next school board election after the school was created, four members were elected to the board, having run their campaign on a platform of getting rid of the superintendent and the school. This happened even though the school had been successful. It won a national award for educational excellence. In addition, academic achievement had gone up, and vandalism had gone down.

We could see that for this school project to survive we needed to communicate with the people who were vehemently opposed to what we were doing. It wasn't easy to get a three-hour meeting with this school board. It took us ten months to arrange the meeting. They wouldn't answer my phone calls, and they wouldn't answer my letters, so I went down to the office once, but they wouldn't see me.

During the ten months we had to find somebody who had access to them, and train this person in our skills so they could try to get a meeting. She finally got them to have the board meet with the school superintendent and me, but they had conditions. They didn't want the press to know about it because it would be embarrassing if they were seen talking with people they got elected to get rid of.

How did Nonviolent Communication help me in that setting? First, I knew I had to do some work on myself before we had that meeting because I had enemy images of this board. I had trouble imagining them as human beings. I had a lot of pain inside because of things they had said about me.

> *I had to do some work on myself because I had enemy images of this board.*

For example, one of the board members owned the local newspaper. I had read an article he wrote about me in which he said, "Are you aware that our 'beloved' superintendent" [he put beloved in quotes because everybody knew he hated the superintendent] "has brought in his Jew again to brainwash our teachers so that they can brainwash our students?" That was only one sample of things I had heard this man had said, so I had a lot to deal with inside.

I also knew that he was head of the local John Birch Society, and I had some inner judgments about people who belonged to that group. I had to do some *despair work*, a very important part of social change.

Despair work is Joanna R. Macy's concept. She's a person working in social change whom I admire very much. She points out how important it is to do despair work, noting that spirituality and social change go together. If we have a good, powerful spirituality, we are much more likely to reach our social-change objectives.

SEEING THE HUMAN BEING
ACROSS THE TABLE

*"Compassion is not religious business, it is
human business, it is not luxury, it is essential
for our own peace and mental stability,
it is essential for human survival."*

— DALAI LAMA

The despair work took this form: I got together with my colleagues on this project the night before our meeting and said to them, "It's going to be hard for me to see this man [the newspaper owner] as a human being tomorrow when we go in there. I've got so much rage inside that I need to do some work on myself."

My team listened empathically to what was going on in me. I had this wonderful opportunity to express my pain and be understood. They could hear the rage I felt—and then, behind the rage, my fear about my hopelessness that we could ever get such people to connect with us in a way that would be good for everyone.

It took three hours the night before the meeting to do all this work, because I had deep pain and a lot of despair. For part of that time I said, "Those of you who have seen him communicate, could we do a little role-playing? I want to try to see his humanness through the way he usually speaks."

I had never seen the man, but they had, and they showed me how he communicated. I worked hard the night before to see his humanness so I wouldn't see him as an enemy. I was glad we did that the night before, because the very next day as we were going into the meeting, he and I happened to be walking through the door at the same time. The first thing he said to me was "This is a waste of time. If you and the school superintendent want to help this community, you'll leave."

My first reaction was wanting to grab him and say, *Look, you said we were going to have a meeting and ... I* took a deep breath. Thank goodness for the despair work the night before.

> *Thank goodness for the despair work the night before.*
>
>

I could get better control over my feelings and try to connect with his humanness. I said, "It sounds like you're feeling kind of hopeless about anything good coming out of this meeting."

He seemed a little surprised that I would try to hear his feelings. He said, "That's right. The project you and the superintendent are doing is destructive to this community. This permissive philosophy of just allowing children to do whatever they want is ridiculous."

Again, I had to take a deep breath, because I was frustrated that he would see it as permissiveness. It showed me that we hadn't made clear what our project was. If he had seen it, he would know we had rules, we had regulations. They weren't set up on the basis of punishment or administered by authorities; they were worked out jointly in the community among the teachers and the students.

I wanted to jump in and get defensive, but I took another

deep breath, and (thanks to the work of the night before) I could see his humanness. So I said to him, "So, it seems you would like some recognition for how important it is to have order in the schools."

He looked at me strangely again, then said, "That's right. You people are menaces. We had great schools in this community before you and the superintendent came."

Again my first reaction was to remind him about all the violence that had been going on in the schools and how the academic achievement had been very low. But I took yet another deep breath and said, "So, it sounds as if there are many things about the schools that you want to support and protect."

I continued to hear what was alive in him and respectfully to connect with his needs.

The meeting went pretty well. He *was* speaking in ways that would have been very easy for me reflect as an enemy image, but after continuing to hear what was alive in him and respectfully trying to connect with his needs, I could see he was better able to open up and understand what we were talking about. I left that meeting feeling quite encouraged.

I went back to my hotel room and felt really good. The phone rang. It was this man, and he said, "You know, I'm sorry I said some things about you in the past. I guess I didn't understand your program. I want to hear more about how you put this together and where you got the ideas." And so forth.

So we talked like brothers for forty minutes on the phone. I poured out to him answers to his questions and my excitement about the school.

Shortly afterward, my colleagues came to pick me up for the airport so I could go home. All the way to the airport I babbled to them about how great it felt. I said, "This is proof of what we're talking about. If you see other people as human beings, you can connect, no matter what or who it is!" I was feeling so good! It reinforced my hopes for social change, that if we can get over this enemy image, we can connect with anybody. Then I told them about the phone call.

The next day a member of my team called me up and said, "Marshall, I've got some bad news for you."

I said, "What's that?"

"We should have warned you. One of this man's tactics is to call people on the phone, and he records what they say, and then he takes portions of it out and uses it to ridicule them in his newspaper. It's an old trick of his; we should have warned you."

Well, I didn't know who I wanted to kill first: him or me. Me, for being so stupid as to trust somebody like that, to think that you can change such a person—or him, for being such a person. I was despondent. By the time it sank in, it was as though he had already done it to me. But, as it turned out, *he didn't do it to me.* And in the

> *A very important part of social change to me is the continual connection to the spiritual energy behind social change.*

next board meeting he voted in favor of our program, even though he had been elected to get rid of it.

That was an important lesson for me in social change. It showed me how it took me three hours the night before to go from my enemy image of the other side—to deal with my pain and the despair about social change—to get myself to a place where I could see the other side as human beings. And it took me five seconds the next day to lose that again on the basis of a rumor.

This is for me a very important part of social change, this continual connection to the spiritual energy that I think needs to be behind social change. And *that* comes from seeing the beauty of what we're for and not the supposed ugliness of the bad guys we're out to conquer.

Transforming Conflict in Business

> *"An argument is the longest distance*
> *between two points of view."*
>
> — Dan Bennett

I'm often asked to mediate conflicts in the corporate world. Companies around the world struggle with infighting and squabbles among their employees. We use NVC to teach companies how to deal with such conflicts. I was brought into one Swiss company that had a departmental conflict that had been going on for fifteen months. They'd been talking about it almost daily. It had to do with which piece of software would be used to do a certain function. But this wasn't a little thing. This was something that involved tens of thousands of dollars, a lot of time, and so forth, to switch from the present software to this new one.

There were two warring factions; one was a younger set and the other an older group. I said, "Whoever wants to start, I'd like to know what needs of yours are not being met in this situation. If we can identify everybody's needs, and everybody can express their needs clearly, I'm certain we'll find strategies for getting everybody's needs met. So, who wants to start?"

After the second word of the first speaker, a member of the older set, I knew why needs weren't being met. I asked for a need, and here's what I heard: "I think that just because something new comes along does not necessarily mean it's effective." He went on, in a long-winded way, to give thoughts justifying the fact that just because something is new doesn't mean it's good. And he gave several examples. And I saw members of the other side looking up at the ceiling because they had heard this for fifteen months.

This being Switzerland, they waited until he finished before they began. (As an aside, that's why I prefer, in some respects, working in the Middle East. Everybody there talks at the same time so you can have the same unproductive discussion in half the time! But maybe that's because that's how my family always did things. In the history of our family, going back centuries, nobody has ever finished a sentence.) Anyway, this being Switzerland, the other faction waited until he finished, and then a member of the younger faction said, "I totally agree with my esteemed colleague about the fact that just because da, da, da, da, da …"

"But I think …" And then he went on.

I let this go on for a while, and then I said, "Has anybody found this meeting productive to this point?"

Not one person had. It was clear to me that there were deep feelings and needs behind those thoughts. As it turned out, with my help, I got the older faction to say how hurt they felt that they weren't getting the recognition for how much the software they had developed had contributed to the organization.

You see, in many of the organizations I've worked with, people can't talk about their feelings. Nobody cares about what you feel and need. It's all about production. But when you don't express your feelings and needs, when you just keep going into intellectual discussions, you end up like this company: unproductive use of time by not getting down to the root of the problem. These older folks were really hurting. But there was no recognition being given to what they had produced. I had to help them. I had to dig this out. It wasn't easy, because in that context people are frightened to reveal their feelings and needs.

I often hear what I heard next: "You can't express your feelings around here. They'll pick you to pieces. They'll think you're weak."

But I got this one group to agree that they were feeling hurt that their needs for recognition weren't being met. I said to the other side, "Would somebody over here just repeat that back so I'm sure this was understood?"

"Well, we understand it, but ..."

"Hold it. Hold it. Please reflect back what he said."

"Well, they think ..."

"No, no, no. Not their thoughts. What are they feeling and needing?"

It wasn't easy. I had to really help them just hear the humanness on the other side. Then I had the younger side express their feelings and needs. They were scared that just because they were young, this new product would not be used. And they were confident it would help. Because they were younger, they felt they weren't receiving respect for their understanding. I got the other side to hear that. Then it didn't take us more than an hour to resolve this fifteen-month-old conflict.

TRANSFORMING BUSINESS CULTURE

"The quality of an organization can never exceed the quality of the minds that make it up."

— HAROLD R. MCALINDON

In many corporations it's not easy to get people to talk at the level of needs and feelings, not to mention that they don't recognize what theologian Walter Wink says is important to know—that every institution, every organization has its own spirituality. And when the spirituality of the organization is "production over all," that's the only thing that counts. Human feelings, human needs, human*ness* doesn't matter. Then the company pays for it in terms of both morale and even production, because when you get people believing that their feelings and needs are understood, production will go up.

Another thing we teach business people is how to do performance evaluations that don't criticize employees when they don't do what supervisors like. In this sense, we teach teachers the same thing. We also teach parents how to evaluate without criticism. I was explaining that to managers in one company. I started by saying something that's part of our training—how to make clear observations, how to get people's attention by expressing what they're doing that you don't like. I asked this group of managers I was with this question: "For example, what behaviors would you like to work on today that are problematic among the employees?"

One said, "Some of these people are just disrespectful of authority."

I said, "Just a minute. That's what I would call a *diagnosis*. I'm asking what they do. You want to evaluate somebody's performance. If you tell them they're disrespectful, you're likely to create a defensive response. What you see is what you get. I would suggest if you want to evaluate people in a way that improves performance, start with a clear observation." He couldn't do it.

Another manager said, "Well, I'm working with employees who are lazy."

I said, "Sorry, that's another diagnosis. It couldn't answer my question about what they *do*."

And one of them finally said, "Darn it, Marshall. This is hard."

As I noted earlier, Krishnamurti says the ability to observe without evaluating is the highest form of human intelligence.

When I was showing them how to make observations, one of the managers jumped up; he literally ran out of the room. The next morning he came in and apologized for his abrupt departure. He said, "You know, yesterday, when you were showing us how to do performance evaluations and how to be sure that you make clear observations and not use any language that sounds like criticism …?"

"Yeah, I remember that."

"The reason I jumped up and ran out on your training yesterday was that while on my way to the training I had stopped at the office and dropped off my performance evaluations for my secretary to type. In the first twenty minutes yesterday you showed me why it's a nightmare of mine every year when it's time for performance evaluations. I can't sleep nights before that time. I know that a significant number of them are going to get hurt and angry. It's going to make matters worse. And you showed me right away that I was confusing observation and evaluation. So I ran back to get my evaluations from the secretary before she typed them up."

He continued: "I was up until 2 a.m. last night trying to figure out how to be clear about what the employees do that I don't like, without mixing in diagnosis or criticism."

When People Won't Meet

*"Leadership has a harder job to do than just
choose sides. It must bring sides together."*

— Jesse Jackson

When it comes down to it, the biggest challenge in social-change efforts—whether in families, corporations, governments, or whatever—is getting people into the room together. I'm serious. This is the biggest challenge.

For example, I was working in a resort in Switzerland where the managers of the kitchen were in conflict with the manager from another area. The owner of the resort wanted a mediation session between these two factions, but they just out-and-out refused to come together. So I met with one of the managers from one of the departments. I played the role of the other department person using Nonviolent Communication. I listened empathically. I expressed in a nonjudgmental way what I had understood the other side's needs were.

We made a tape recording of this. With this person's permission I took the tape to the other side, played it, and then I did the same thing for the other side. I did all of this just to see if I could get them both into a room together, but just by doing that much we already resolved the conflict. None of this would have happened if I hadn't used a creative way of "getting them into the same room."

CHAPTER · 12

GRATITUDE

"Gratitude unlocks the fullness of life.
It turns what we have into enough, and more.
It turns denial into acceptance, chaos to order,
confusion to clarity. It can turn a meal into a feast,
a house into a home, a stranger into a friend.
Gratitude makes sense of our past, brings peace
for today, and creates a vision for tomorrow."

— MELODIE BEATTIE

GRATITUDE IS ANOTHER VITAL PART OF SOCIAL CHANGE, but it's also important in helping to sustain a kind of spiritual consciousness that Nonviolent Communication tries to support. When we know how to express and receive gratitude in a certain way, it gives us enormous energy to sustain our social-change efforts, as well as to sustain us through the beauty of what can be, rather than attempting to conquer evil forces.

I first got a good dose of how important gratitude can be by working with a powerful feminist group in Iowa. I admired their work and felt honored that they wanted me to show them how Nonviolent Communication might help them in their social-change efforts. But one thing was driving me a little batty in my three days with them. Each day they would stop at least a couple of times to express gratitude, to celebrate things they wanted to celebrate. And at that time I was so preoccupied with how much needed to be done in the world that this was very frustrating for me, to stop a meeting just to celebrate. There's so much racism, sexism, so much that needed to change, and I was so absorbed with what needed to be done that I didn't have much room for celebration.

So, on the third evening after our work was done, I was having dinner with the leader of the group, and she said, "What was it like working with our organization?"

And I said, "I admire very much what you folks are getting done. It was a pleasure to be here. One thing that was a little awkward for me, though, was how often you stop to celebrate and give thanks. I'm just not used to that."

And she said, "I'm glad you brought that up, Marshall. That's something I wanted to talk to you about. Aren't you worried about any social-change effort that's just so preoccupied with how horrible things are that you come from *that* energy, rather than reminding yourself constantly of the beautiful side of life? That's why we do gratitude in our social-change efforts. Even though we know there's so much to be done, we want to stop and be grateful for whatever people are doing that is successfully supporting what we're working toward."

That started me thinking of how much my consciousness had been shaped by how bad things are and how much needs to be done. This was creating a pretty scary guy in me. And from that point to the present, which as been about thirty years now, I have been working hard to build the expression of gratitude into our training of Nonviolent Communication. We see how it can sustain our living in harmony with our spiritual values. The more we express and receive gratitude in a certain way, the more it reminds us of the spirituality that Nonviolent Communication tries to support.

As I've said, the spirituality we embrace is to make people conscious moment by moment that our purpose in life comes from compassionate giving, compassionate service. There's nothing more wonderful than exercising our power in the service of life. That's a manifestation of the divine energy within us, and that is our greatest joy: to use our efforts in the service of life.

PRAISE AND COMPLIMENTS AS DAMAGING JUDGMENTS

"When two people relate to each other authentically and humanly, God is the electricity that surges between them."

— MARTIN BUBER

We show people how to express and receive gratitude in Nonviolent Communication in a way that helps us sustain our lives in harmony with that spirituality. But that means being conscious of how we have been taught to express gratitude in ways that are directly counter to supporting that kind of spirituality. In Nonviolent Communication we suggest not giving compliments or praise. In my view, telling somebody they did a good job, that they're a kind or competent person ... that's still using moralistic judgments. That's still creating a world different from the world Rumi is talking about when he says there's a place beyond rightdoing and wrongdoing. When we're using judgmental words for praise and compliments, it's the same *form* of language as telling somebody they're unkind, stupid, or selfish.

We suggest that positive judgments are equally as dehumanizing to people as negative judgments. We also suggest how destructive it is to give positive feedback as a reward. Don't dehumanize people by complimenting them or praising them. When I say this to managers in industry or to teachers, they're often shocked. They've often been in training programs that teach them to compliment and praise employees or students daily because performance rises. And I point out to such people that if you look at the research you will see that, yes, most children work harder when they're praised and complimented. Most employees work harder when they're praised and complimented ... but only for a very short time. It lasts until they sense the manipulation, until they sense that this is not the real stuff, that this is not gratitude from the heart. That is another manipulation, another way of trying to get them to do things. And when people sense the manipulation, the production no longer stays high.

If you want to read more about the violence of rewards, to see that it's the same kind of violence as punishment, and just as dangerous, read Alfie Kohn's book, *Punished by Rewards: The Trouble with Gold Stars, Incentive Plans, A's, Praise, and Other Bribes.* Both punishment and praise are means of control over people. In Nonviolent Communication we want to increase power, but power *with* people, not over them.

Expressing Gratitude with NVC

*"In our daily lives, we must see that it is not
happiness that makes us grateful, but the
gratefulness that makes us happy."*

— Albert Clarke

How do we express gratitude in Nonviolent Communication? First, the intent is all-important: to celebrate life, nothing else. We're not trying to reward the other person. We want the other person to know how our life has been enriched by what they did. That's our only intent. To make clear how our life has been enriched, we need to say three things to people, and praise and compliments don't make these three things clear:

- First, we want to make clear what the person did that we want to celebrate, what action on their part enriched our lives.

- Second, we want to tell them how we feel about that, what feelings are alive in us as a result of what they've done.

- Third, we want to tell them what needs of ours were met by their actions.

I hadn't made this clear to a group of teachers I was dealing with. We ran out of time one day just as I was talking about how to express gratitude in Nonviolent Communication. After the meeting one of the teachers ran up to me, and here's how she expressed her gratitude to me. Her eyes were shining, and she said, "You're brilliant."

I said to her, "That doesn't help."

She said, "What?"

I said, "Telling me what I am doesn't help. I have been called a lot of names in my life. Some positive and some far from positive, and I can't ever recall learning anything of value by somebody telling me what I am. I don't think anybody does. I think there's zero information value in being told what you are. But from the look in your eyes, I can see you want to express gratitude."

Looking a bit bewildered, she said, "Yes."

"And I want to receive it. But telling me what I am doesn't give it to me."

"Well," she said, "what do you want me to say?"

I said, "Remember what I said in the workshop today? I need to hear three things. First of all, what did I do that made life more wonderful for you?"

She thought for a moment and said, "You're so intelligent."

"No," I said, "that's still a diagnosis of me. It doesn't really tell me what I did. I'd get more out of your feedback if I knew concretely what I did that really in some way enriched your life."

"Oh," she said, "I got you. I think I understand." She opened up her notebook and she pointed to two things she wrote there that had big stars by them. She said, "You said these two things."

I looked in her notebook. "Yes, that helps, just knowing that I in some way enriched your life. Second," I continued, "it would help me to know how you feel right now."

"Oh, Marshall, I feel so relieved and hopeful."

"OK. And now third, what need of yours was met by those two things?"

"Marshall, I've never been able to connect with my eighteen-year-old son. All we do is fight. I needed some concrete direction for connecting with him. These two things you said met that need of mine for some concrete direction."

I said, "Thank you for sticking with me and helping me see how I have contributed to you. It is so much more satisfying for me to know concretely what I did."

You can see, I'm sure, how different it was to hear those three things than to hear somebody tell me what I was. That's how we express gratitude in Nonviolent Communication.

HOW TO RECEIVE GRATITUDE

"Let us be grateful to people who make us happy;
they are the charming gardeners who
make our souls blossom."

— MARCEL PROUST

Now I'd like to suggest how to receive gratitude in Nonviolent Communication. We find in every country how hard it is for people to receive gratitude, because their prior training has taught them that you should be humble, you shouldn't think you're anything. It's very hard for people to receive gratitude.

For example, people who speak English. They often look terrified when you express gratitude to them. Here's what they say: "Oh, it's nothing. It's nothing. It's nothing." French people say it, Hispanic people say it, Swedish people say it. All over the world I've asked people, "What makes it so hard to receive gratitude?"

Here's the answer I get: "Well, I didn't know that I deserved it." It's the horrible concept of *deserve*. We have to earn things. It makes it hard even to receive gratitude when you have to worry about whether or not you earned it.

Or sometimes they'll say, "Well, what's wrong with being humble?"

And I answer, "It depends on what you mean by humility. There are different kinds of humility. There's one kind that I think is unfortunate, because it deprives us of seeing our power, our beauty."

I like the way former Israeli Prime Minister Golda Meir talked about this false humility to one of her politicians. She said to him once, "Don't be so humble, you're not that great." And I think the most important reason people find it hard to receive gratitude is powerfully spelled out in *A Course in Miracles* (published by Foundation for Inner Peace), which says it's our light, not our darkness, that scares us the most.

Sadly, we've been educated for all these years in this world of moralistic judgments; of retributive justice; of punishment, reward, and "deserve." We've internalized this language of judgments, and it's hard for us to stay connected to the beauty of what we are within that framework.

Nonviolent Communication shows us how to have the courage to face the power and the beauty that is within each of us.

CHAPTER · 13

SUMMARY/FINAL THOUGHTS

*"Mankind must evolve for all human conflict a method
which rejects revenge, aggression, and retaliation.
The foundation of such a method is love."*

— MARTIN LUTHER KING JR.

I N THIS BOOK WE HAVE LOOKED AT CREATING PEACE BY
connecting to life at three levels—and how each of us can
learn to do that.

- First, within ourselves, how we can connect to the
  life within ourselves so we can learn from our
  limitations without blaming and punishing
  ourselves. Our training shows people how to create
  peace within themselves. If we can't do that, I'm
  not too optimistic how we're going to relate
  peacefully out in the world.

- Second, how to create life-enriching connections

with other people that allows compassionate giving
to take place naturally.

- Third, how to transform the structures we've
  created—corporate, judicial, governmental, and
  others—that don't support peaceful, life-enriching
  connections between us.

Our training shows people how to function at all three of
these levels: within ourselves, with other people, and with
structures that can support and create compassionate giving.

I hope you will realize that we need a different economic
system than the one we have now, not just in this country but
internationally. I hope you read what David Korten has to offer
in his books *The Post-Corporate World* and *When Corporations
Rule the World*, Paul Hawken's *Natural Capitalism*, and
Margaret Wheatley's work. I hope you will see that there are
other economic systems possible—systems that can greatly
increase peace and protect this planet. I fervently hope that you
also will see these systems are within our grasp, and that you
will join our work toward this goal.

Further, I would hope that you become familiar with
restorative justice. Our judicial system is catastrophic. It
creates more violence than it prevents, yet most people can
only perceive a choice between anarchy and our present
system. We think if we're not going to punish people and kill
people that we're going to have anarchy. I hope you realize
that there are more powerful ways of creating judicial systems

based on restorative justice that would be safer for us all.

So, those would be two things I would hope everybody would become familiar with:

- Radically different economic systems.

- Judicial systems different from the ones that are presently creating great pain on our planet.

I believe, as did Teilhard de Chardin, that a peaceful world is not only possible, it's inevitable. I think we're evolving in that direction. Of course, he was very patient because he was a paleontologist; he thought in terms of tens of thousands of years. And he wasn't naïve about all the violence that's going on now, but he saw the violence as just an evolutionary snag. He sees our evolution and I do, too, but I'm not as patient as he is. I can't wait thousands of years for it, so I'm interested in how we can speed it up. But I think it's inevitable and, unless we destroy the planet in the meantime, I think we're moving in that direction.

I, along with my associates at the Center for Nonviolent Communication, will continue to provide this education for people so they can create a world within themselves that will support and sustain an outer world of peace. We do this because we want people to know how to create peace in their relationships—and also know the power they have to create structures that support compassionate interactions, compassionate exchanges of resources, and compassionate justice.

BIBLIOGRAPHY

Baran, Josh (ed.). *365 Nirvana Here and Now: Living Every Moment in Enlightenment* (ThorsonsElement, Apr. 2005)

Domhoff, G. William. *Who Rules America? Power and Politics* (McGraw-Hill; 4th edition, Jun. 2001)

Hawken, Paul. *Natural Capitalism: Creating the Next Industrial Revolution* (Back Bay Books; 1st edition, Oct. 2000)

Katz, Michael B. *Class, Bureaucracy, and Schools: The Illusion of Educational Change in America* (Praeger Publishers, Jan. 1975)

Kohn, Alfie. *Punished by Rewards: The Trouble with Gold Stars, Incentive Plans, A's, Praise, and Other Bribes* (Mariner Books, Sep. 1999)

Korten, David. *The Post-Corporate World: Life After Capitalism* (Berrett-Koehler Publishers; 1st edition, Sep. 2000)

Korten, David. *When Corporations Rule the World* (Berrett-Koehler Publishers; 2nd edition, May 2001)

Macy, Joanna R. *Coming Back to Life: Practices to Reconnect Our Lives, Our World* (New Society Publishers, Oct. 1998)

Szasz, Thomas. *The Myth of Mental Illness: Foundations of a Theory of Personal Conduct* (Perennial Currents, Nov. 1984)

Wink, Walter. *The Powers That Be* (Galilee Trade, Mar. 1999)

Wheatley, Margaret J. *Finding Our Way: Leadership for an Uncertain Time* (Berrett-Koehler Publishers; Feb. 2005)

Wheatley, Margaret J. *Turning to One Another: Simple Conversations to Restore Hope to the Future* (Berrett-Koehler Publishers, Jan. 2002)

INDEX

meetings, increasing
effectiveness of, 134–36,
146, 155–57
men, and denial of needs, 44,
106
mental illness and education,
67
messages of others,
responding to needs in,
76–86, 87–93, 118–25,
138–40, 151–52
minority citizens, and social
change, 134–40
mistakes
identifying unmet needs,
63–66
self-blame and, 60–62
self-empathy for, 65–71
moralistic judgments. *See*
judgments
motivators in authority-
based systems, 28–29,
35–36, 61
mourning our actions,
62–63, 65, 71–74, 103
multinational corporations
as gangs, 107, 110–11
social change in, 127–30
The Myth of Mental Illness
(Szasz), 67

N

Natural Capitalism
(Hawken), 172
natural suffering, 73–74
nature of humans, 13–14,
16–18, 28
need consciousness, 105
needs
as basis of behavior, 11,
63–66, 68–71, 73–74,
96–102
as cause of feelings, 35
empathic connection with
others', 77–86, 151–52
in expression of gratitude,
166–68
fear of expressing, 79,
156–57
identifying, 37–39
in messages of others,
87–93, 118–25, 138–39
mistakes and, 68–71, 74
social change and, 127–30
vocabulary of, 44, 188
negative focus in social
change work, 161–63
Nigeria, NVC in, 121–25
"no," fear of hearing, 79–80
non-responders to NVC,
91–92
nonverbal connection with
another, 90–91
Nonviolent Communication
schools, 90, 111

Some Basic Feelings We All Have

Feelings when needs "are" fulfilled

- Amazed
- Confident
- Energetic
- Glad
- Inspired

- Joyous
- Optimistic
- Relieved
- Surprised
- Touched

- Comfortable
- Eager
- Fulfilled
- Hopeful
- Intrigued

- Moved
- Proud
- Stimulated
- Thankful
- Trustful

Feelings when needs "are not" fulfilled

- Angry
- Confused
- Disappointed
- Distressed
- Frustrated

- Hopeless
- Irritated
- Nervous
- Puzzled
- Sad

- Annoyed
- Concerned
- Discouraged
- Embarrassed
- Helpless

- Impatient
- Lonely
- Overwhelmed
- Reluctant
- Uncomfortable

Some Basic Needs We All Have

Autonomy
- Choosing dreams/goals/values
- Choosing plans for fulfilling one's dreams, goals, values

Celebration
- Celebrate the creation of life and dreams fulfilled
- Celebrate losses: loved ones, dreams, etc. (mourning)

Integrity
- Authenticity • Creativity
- Meaning • Self-worth

Interdependence
- Acceptance • Appreciation
- Closeness • Community
- Consideration
- Contribute to the enrichment of life
- Emotional Safety • Empathy

Physical Nurturance
- Air • Food
- Movement, exercise
- Protection from life-threatening forms of life: viruses, bacteria, insects, predatory animals
- Rest • Sexual expression
- Shelter • Touch • Water

Play
- Fun • Laughter

Spiritual Communion
- Beauty • Harmony
- Inspiration • Order • Peace

- Honesty (the empowering honesty that enables us to learn from our limitations)
- Love • Reassurance
- Respect • Support
- Trust • Understanding

How You Can Use the NVC Process

Clearly expressing how **I am** without blaming or criticizing	Empathically receiving how **you are** without hearing blame or criticism

OBSERVATIONS

1. What I observe *(see, hear, remember, imagine, free from my evaluations)* that does or does not contribute to my well-being:

   "When I (see, hear) . . . "

1. What you observe *(see, hear, remember, imagine, free from your evaluations)* that does or does not contribute to your well-being:

   "When you see/hear . . . "

   (Sometimes dropped when offering empathy)

FEELINGS

2. How I feel *(emotion or sensation rather than thought)* in relation to what I observe:

   "I feel . . . "

2. How you feel *(emotion or sensation rather than thought)* in relation to what you observe:

   "You feel . . ."

NEEDS

3. What I need or value *(rather than a preference, or a specific action)* that causes my feelings:

   " . . . because I need/value . . . "

3. What you need or value *(rather than a preference, or a specific action)* that causes your feelings:

   " . . . because you need/value . . ."

Clearly requesting that which would enrich **my** life without demanding	Empathically receiving that which would enrich **your** life without hearing any demand

REQUESTS

4. The concrete actions I would like taken:

   "Would you be willing to . . . ?"

4. The concrete actions you would like taken:

   "Would you like . . . ?"

   (Sometimes dropped when offering empathy)

About CNVC

The Center for Nonviolent Communication (CNVC) is an international nonprofit peacemaking organization whose vision is a world where everyone's needs are met peacefully. CNVC is devoted to supporting the spread of Nonviolent Communication (NVC) around the world.

Founded in 1984 by Dr. Marshall B. Rosenberg, CNVC has been contributing to a vast social transformation in thinking, speaking and acting—showing people how to connect in ways that inspire compassionate results. Around the globe, training in NVC is now being taught in communities, schools, prisons, mediation centers, churches, businesses, professional conferences and more. Dr. Rosenberg spends more than 250 days each year teaching NVC in some of the most impoverished, war-torn states of the world. More than 180 certified trainers and hundreds more teach NVC in 35 countries to approximately 250,000 people each year.

At CNVC we believe that NVC training is a crucial step to continue building a compassionate, peaceful society. Your tax-deductible donation will help CNVC continue to provide training in some of the most impoverished, violent corners of the world. It will also support the development and continuation of organized projects aimed at bringing NVC training to high-need geographic regions and populations.

To make a tax-deductible donation or to learn more about the valuable resources described below, visit the CNVC website at www.CNVC.org

- **Training and Certification** – Find local, national and international training opportunities, access trainer certification information, connect to local NVC communities, trainers and more.

- **CNVC Bookstore** – Find mail or phone order information for a complete selection of NVC books, booklets, audio and video materials at the CNVC website.

- **CNVC Projects** – Seven regional and theme-based projects provide focus and leadership for teaching NVC in a particular application or geographic region. Get involved or learn more on our website.

- **Network News** – To receive our annual printed newsletter, Network News, register on our website as a local supporter via our secure, private database.

- **E-Groups and List Servs** – Join one of several moderated, topic-based NVC e-groups and list servs developed to support individual learning and the continued growth of NVC worldwide.

For more information, please contact CNVC at:

 2428 Foothill Blvd., Suite E • La Crescenta, CA 91214
Phone: 818-957-9393 • Fax: 818-957-1424
Email: cnvc@cnvc.org • www.cnvc.org

About NVC

From the bedroom to the boardroom, from the classroom to the war zone, Nonviolent Communication (NVC) is changing lives every day. NVC provides an easy to grasp, effective method to get to the root of violence and pain peacefully. By examining the unmet needs behind what we do or say, NVC helps reduce hostility, heal pain, and strengthen professional and personal relationships. NVC is now being taught in corporations, classrooms, prisons, and mediation centers worldwide. And it is affecting cultural shifts as institutions, corporations, and governments integrate NVC consciousness into their organizational structures and their approach to leadership.

Most of us are hungry for skills that can improve the quality of our relationships, to deepen our sense of personal empowerment or simply help us communicate more effectively. Unfortunately, most of us have been educated from birth to compete, judge, demand and diagnose; to think and communicate in terms of what is "right" and "wrong" with people. At best, the habitual ways we think and speak hinder communication and create misunderstanding or frustration. And still worse, they can cause anger and pain, and may lead to violence. Without wanting to, even people with the best of intentions generate needless conflict.

NVC helps us reach beneath the surface and discover what is alive and vital within us, and how all of our actions are based on human needs that we are seeking to meet. We learn to develop a vocabulary of feelings and needs that helps us more clearly express what is going on in us at any given moment. When we understand and acknowledge our needs, we develop a shared foundation for much more satisfying relationships. Join the thousands of people worldwide who have improved their relationships and their lives with this simple yet revolutionary process.

About PuddleDancer Press

PuddleDancer Press (PDP) is the premier publisher of Nonviolent Communication™ related works. Its mission is to provide high quality materials that help people create a world in which all needs are met compassionately. PDP is the unofficial marketing arm of the international Center for Nonviolent Communication. Publishing revenues are used to develop and implement NVC promotion, educational materials and media campaigns. By working in partnership with CNVC, NVC trainers, teams and local supporters, PDP has created a comprehensive, cost-effective promotion effort that has helped bring NVC to thousands more people each year.

Since 2003, PDP has donated over 50,000 NVC books to organizations, decision-makers and individuals in need around the world. This program is supported in part by donations to CNVC, and by partnerships with like-minded organizations around the world. To ensure the continuation of this program, please make a tax-deductible donation to CNVC, earmarked to the Book Giveaway Campaign at www.CNVC.org/donation

Visit the PDP website at www.NonviolentCommunication.com to find the following resources:

- **Shop NVC** — Continue your learning—purchase our NVC titles online safely and conveniently. Find multiple-copy and package discounts, learn more about our authors and read dozens of book endorsements from renowned leaders, educators, relationship experts and more.

- **e-Newsletter** — To stay apprised of new titles and the impact NVC is having around the globe, visit our website and register for the quarterly NVC Quick Connect e-Newsletter. Archived newsletters are also available.

- **Help Share NVC** — Access hundreds of valuable tools, resources and adaptable documents to help you share NVC, form a local NVC community, coordinate NVC workshops and trainings, and promote the life-enriching benefits of NVC training to organizations and communities in your area. Sign up for our NVC Promotion e-Bulletin to get all the latest tips and tools.

- **For the Press** — Journalists and producers can access author bios and photos, recently published articles in the media, video clips and other valuable information.

- **Help Share NVC Community Forum** — Scheduled for launch in mid-2005, the Help Share NVC Community Forum provides an online space to support the continued growth and spread of NVC worldwide. Join our forum today at www.ShareNVC.com

For more information, please contact PuddleDancer Press at:

P.O. Box 231129 • Encinitas CA 92024
Phone: 858-759-6963 • Fax: 858-759-6967
Email: email@puddledancer.com • www.NonviolentCommunication.com

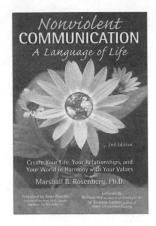

Nonviolent Communication:
A Language of Life, Second Edition

Create Your Life, Your Relationships and
Your World in Harmony with Your Values

Marshall B. Rosenberg, Ph.D.

$17.95 — Trade Paper 5-3/8x8-3/8, 240pp
ISBN: 1-892005-03-4

Most of us are hungry for skills to improve the quality of our relationships, to deepen our sense of personal empowerment or to simply communicate more effectively. In this internationally acclaimed text, Marshall Rosenberg offers insightful stories, anecdotes, practical exercises and role-plays that will literally change your approach to communication for the better. Discover how the language you use can strengthen your relationships, build trust, prevent conflicts and heal pain. Revolutionary, yet simple, NVC offers the most effective tools to reduce violence and create peace—one interaction at a time.

Over 150,000 copies of this landmark book have been sold. Printed in 20 languages around the globe.

"Unless, as grandfather would say, 'we become the change we wish to see in the world,' no change will ever take place . . . If we change ourselves we can change the world, and changing ourselves begins with changing our language and methods of communication. I highly recommend reading this book and applying the Nonviolent Communication process it teaches."

> — **Foreword by Arun Gandhi**, *grandson of Mahatma Gandhi and*
> *co-founder of the M.K. Gandhi Institute for Nonviolence*

"Nonviolent communication is a simple yet powerful methodology for communicating in a way that meets both parties' needs. This is one of the most useful books you will ever read."

> — **William Ury**, co-author of *Getting to Yes* and author of *The Third Side*

"I believe the principles and techniques in this book can literally change the world, but more importantly, they can change the quality of your life with your spouse, your children, your neighbors, your coworkers and everyone else you interact with."

> — **Jack Canfield**, author, *Chicken Soup for the Soul*

Available from PDP, CNVC, all major bookstores and Amazon.com
Distributed by IPG: 800-888-4741

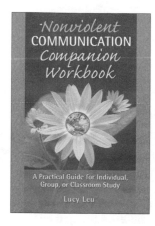

Nonviolent Communication Companion Workbook

A Practical Guide for Individual, Group or Classroom Study

by Lucy Leu

$19.95 – Trade Paper 7x10, 224pp
ISBN: 1-892005-04-2

Learning Nonviolent Communication has often been equated with learning a whole new language. The *NVC Companion Workbook* helps you put these powerful, effective skills into practice with chapter-by-chapter study of Rosenberg's cornerstone text, *NVC: A Language of Life.*

An exceptional resource for:

- **Individuals**—Integrate the liberating practice of the NVC process in your daily life as the workbook guides you through self-directed study.

- **Group Practice**—Find structured guidance for practice facilitation including group process suggestions, customizable activities and ideas for handling common group challenges.

- **Educators**—Find everything you need to develop your own NVC course or to augment any existing curriculum including an extensive reference and resource section.

"I've used this workbook now in two prison facilities. It has been a wonderful tool for men and women who are committed to gaining useful life skills in some of the toughest of environments."

> — **Karen Campbell**, *workforce/lifeskills coordinator,*
> *Coffee Creek Corrections Facility*

"We went over real-life situations and followed various exercises that promoted understanding the content more fully. This practice was the key for my success in understanding and using NVC!"

> — **Kirsten Ingram**, *finance and administration officer,*
> *Children's Commission Province of British Columbia*

Available from PDP, CNVC, all major bookstores and Amazon.com
Distributed by IPG: 800-888-4741

NEW!
Peaceful Living

Daily Meditations for Living with Love, Healing and Compassion

by Mary Mackenzie

$15.95 – Trade Paper 5x7.5, 390pp
ISBN: 1-892005-19-0

Live More Authentically and Peacefully than you Ever Dreamed Possible—In this gathering of wisdom, Mary Mackenzie empowers you to change the course of your life for the better. With each of the 366 daily meditations you will learn new ways of viewing familiar, everyday situations and discover tools to transform those situations into opportunities for connection and personal growth.

Peaceful Living goes beyond daily affirmations, providing the skills and consciousness you need to transform relationships, heal pain, and discover the life-enriching meaning behind even the most trying situations. Begin each day centered and connected to yourself and your values. Direct the course of your life toward your deepest hopes and needs. Ground yourself in the power of compassionate, conscious living.

Discover the life-enriching benefits of *Peaceful Living:*

- Create an empowered, purposeful life free of fear, shame or guilt

- Deepen your emotional connections with your partner, colleagues, family and friends

- Hear the needs behind whatever anyone does or says

- Transform judgment and criticism into understanding and connection

Available from PDP, CNVC, all major bookstores and Amazon.com
Distributed by IPG: 800-888-4741

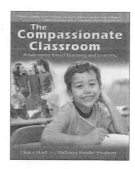

The Compassionate Classroom
Relationship Based Teaching and Learning
by Sura Hart and Victoria Kindle Hodson

$17.95 – Trade Paper 7.5x9.25, 208pp
ISBN: 1-892005-06-9

When compassion thrives, so does learning—Learn powerful skills to create an emotionally safe learning environment where academic excellence thrives. Build trust, reduce conflict, improve cooperation and maximize the potential of each student as you create relationship-centered classrooms. This how-to guide offers customizable exercises, activities, charts and cutouts that make it easy for educators to create lesson plans for a day, a week or an entire school year. An exceptional resource for educators, homeschool parents, child care providers and mentors.

"Education is not simply about teachers covering a curriculum; it is a dance of relationships. The Compassionate Classroom presents both the case for teaching compassionately, and a wide range of practical tools to maximize student potential."

— **Tim Seldin**, *president, The Montessori Foundation*

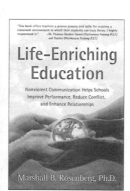

Life-Enriching Education
Nonviolent Communication Helps Schools Improve Performance, Reduce Conflict, and Enhance Relationships

by Marshall B. Rosenberg, Ph.D.

$12.95 – Tade Paper 5-3/8x8-3/8, 192pp
ISBN: 1-892005-05-0

Filled with insight, adaptable exercises and role-plays, *Life-Enriching Education* gives educators practical skills to generate mutually respectful classroom relationships. Discover how our language and organizational structures directly impact student potential, trust, self-esteem and student enjoyment in their learning. Rediscover the joy of teaching in a classroom where each person's needs are respected!

NVC will empower you to:
- Get to the heart of classroom conflicts quickly
- Listen so students are really heard
- Maximize the individual potential of all students
- Strengthen student interest, retention and connection to their school work
- Improve trust and connection in your classroom community
- Let go of unhealthy, coercive teaching styles
- Improve classroom teamwork, efficiency and cooperation

Available from PDP, CNVC, all major bookstores and Amazon.com
Distributed by IPG: 800-888-4741

195

Trade Booklets from PuddleDancer Press

NEW! Being Me, Loving You • *A Practical Guide to Extraordinary Relationships* by **Marshall B. Rosenberg, Ph.D.** • Discover the "how-to" of heart to heart connections strengthened by joyfully giving and receiving. 80pp, ISBN: 1-892005-16-6 • **$6.95**

NEW! Eat by Choice, Not by Habit • *Practical Skills for Creating a Healthy Relationship with Your Body and Food* **by Sylvia Haskvitz** • Let NVC help you uncover the missing link in your relationship with your body and food. 128pp, ISBN: 1-892005-20-4 • **$8.95**

Getting Past the Pain Between Us • *Healing and Reconciliation Without Compromise* by **Marshall B. Rosenberg, Ph.D.** • Learn the healing power of listening and speaking from the heart. Skills for resolving conflicts, healing old hurts, and reconciling strained relationships. 48pp, ISBN: 1-892005-07-7 • **$6.95**

The Heart of Social Change • *How to Make a Difference in Your World* **by Marshall B. Rosenberg, Ph.D.** • Learn how creating an internal consciousness of compassion can impact your social change efforts. 48pp, ISBN: 1-892005-10-7 • **$6.95**

Parenting From Your Heart • *Sharing the Gifts of Compassion, Connection, and Choice* **by Inbal Kashtan** • Addresses the challenges of parenting with real-world solutions for creating family relationships that meet everyone's needs. 48pp, ISBN: 1-892005-08-5 • **$6.95**

NEW! Practical Spirituality • *Reflections on the Spiritual Basis of Nonviolent Communication* **by Marshall B. Rosenberg, Ph.D.** • Marshall's views on the spiritual origins and underpinnings of NVC, and how practicing the process helps him connect to the Divine. 48pp, ISBN: 1-892005-14-X • **$6.95**

Raising Children Compassionately • *Parenting the Nonviolent Communication Way* by **Marshall B. Rosenberg, Ph.D.** • Filled with insight and stories, this booklet will prove invaluable to parents, teachers, and others who want to nurture children and themselves. 32pp, ISBN: 1-892005-09-3 • **$5.95**

NEW! The Surprising Purpose of Anger • *Beyond Anger Management: Finding the Gift* by **Marshall B. Rosenberg, Ph.D.** • Learn the key truths about what anger is really telling us. Use it to uncover your needs and get them met in constructive ways. 48pp, ISBN: 1-892005-15-8 • **$6.95**

Teaching Children Compassionately • *How Students and Teachers Can Succeed with Mutual Understanding* by **Marshall B. Rosenberg, Ph.D.** • Skills for creating a successful classroom—from a keynote address and workshop given to a national conference of Montessori educators. 48pp, ISBN: 1-892005-11-5 • **$6.95**

We Can Work It Out • *Resolving Conflicts Peacefully and Powerfully* **by Marshall B. Rosenberg, Ph.D.** • Practical suggestions for fostering empathic connection, genuine cooperation, and satisfying resolutions in even the most difficult situations. 32pp, ISBN: 1-892005-12-3 • **$5.95**

What's Making You Angry? • *10 Steps to Transforming Anger So Everyone Wins* by **Shari Klein and Neill Gibson** • A step-by-step guide to re-focus your attention when you're angry, and create outcomes that are satisfying for everyone. 32pp, ISBN: 1-892005-13-1 • **$5.95**

Available from PDP, CNVC, all major bookstores and Amazon.com. Distributed by IPG: 800-888-4741. For more information about these booklets or to order online visit www.NonviolentCommunication.com

NVC Materials Available from CNVC

Available from the Center for Nonviolent Communication
at www.CNVC.org or call 800-255-7696.

The Giraffe Classroom **$18**
by Nancy Sokol Green • 8.5x11, 122pp, (spiral bound) • Humorous, creative, and
thought provoking activities. Ideal for teachers, parents, and anyone who wants to
use concrete exercises to learn the process of NVC.

Communication Basics **$4**
An Overview of Nonviolent Communication (24pp)
by Rachelle Lamb • This new booklet provides a clear, concise, and handy summary
of what one might learn in an introductory training in Nonviolent Communication.

Nonviolent Communication **$10**
The Basics as I Know and Use Them (4x7, 94pp)
by Wayland Myers, Ph.D • A clear, compassionate, simple and practical presentation
of NVC applied interpersonally.

The Basics of Nonviolent Communication **$50**
An Introductory Training (2 videotapes, 3hrs)
by Marshall B. Rosenberg, Ph.D. • This edited one-day training shows how we can
connect with others in a way that enables everyone's needs to be met through
natural giving.

Making Life Wonderful **$100**
An Intermediate Training (4 videotapes, over 8hrs)
by Marshall B. Rosenberg, Ph.D. • Improve relationships with self and others by
increasing fluency in NVC. Two-day training session in San Francisco filled with
insights, examples, extended role-plays, stories, and songs that will deepen your
grasp of NVC.

THESE AND ADDITIONAL MATERIALS AVAILABLE AT:
(10% Member Discount available—Prices may change.)

Mail: CNVC, 2428 Foothill Blvd., Suite E, La Crescenta, CA 91214
Phone: 800-255-7696 (toll free order line) or by Fax: 1-818-957-1424
Shipping: Call 1-818-957-9393 to determine actual shipping charges.
Please pay with US dollars only.

Contributions and Membership: A contribution of $35 or more qualifies you as
a member of CNVC and entitles you to a 10% discount on CNVC materials ordered
from the Center. Your tax-deductible contribution of any amount will be gratefully
received and will help support CNVC projects worldwide.

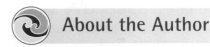

About the Author

Photo by Beth Banning

Marshall B. Rosenberg, Ph.D. is the founder and director of educational services for the Center for Nonviolent Communication, an international peacemaking organization. He is the author of *Speak Peace in a World of Conflict*, and the bestselling *Nonviolent Communication: A Language of Life*. Dr. Rosenberg is the 2006 recipient of the Global Village Foundation's Bridge of Peace Award, and the Association of Unity Churches International 2006 Light of God Expressing Award. Rosenberg spends more than 250 days each year traveling the globe, teaching Nonviolent Communication (NVC) in hundreds of local communities, at national conferences, and in some of the most impoverished, war-torn states of the world.

Growing up in a turbulent Detroit neighborhood, Dr. Rosenberg developed a keen interest in new forms of communication that would provide peaceful alternatives to the violence he encountered. His interest led to a doctorate in clinical psychology from the University of Wisconsin in 1961, where he studied under Carl Rogers. His subsequent life experience and study of comparative religion motivated him to develop the Nonviolent Communication (NVC) process.

Dr. Rosenberg first used the NVC process in federally funded school integration projects to provide mediation and communication skills training during the 1960s. He founded the Center for Nonviolent Communication in 1984, an international nonprofit peacemaking organization, which is now affiliated with more than 180 certified NVC trainers in 35 countries around the globe.

With guitar and puppets in hand, a history of traveling to some of the most violent corners of the world, and a spiritual energy that fills a room, Rosenberg shows us how to create a much more peaceful and satisfying world. Dr. Rosenberg is currently based in Wasserfallenhof, Switzerland.